Praise for
HOW'S YOUR FAITH?

"David Gregory has taken on the most fundamental of questions in this thoughtful and engaging book about the deepening of one's faith in an invisible order amid the hurly-burly of the visible world. The result is an honest and bracing account of a good man's struggle to be an even better man—with God's help. I learned a lot from *How's Your Faith?* and you will, too."

—Jon Meacham, Pulitzer Prize–winning
author of *American Gospel*

"A thoughtful, introspective, and moving account. This is a book for seekers of faith."

—*The Washington Post*

"An unusual, probing book, part memoir, part cri de coeur, part exploration."

—*The Boston Globe*

"In eloquent but everyday language, David Gregory introduces us to his ever-deepening faith. A spiritual journey that is honest, humble, and elevating."

—Rabbi David J. Wolpe,
author of *Why Faith Matters*

"Genuine and deeply felt."

—*The Wall Street Journal*

"His experience in journalism made Gregory approach faith in an investigative manner."

—*The Christian Post*

"Gregory's vulnerability in sharing the lessons he learned . . . distinguishes this book in the crowded lineup of spiritual-seeking memoirs."

—*Bookpage*

How's Your Faith?

AN UNLIKELY
SPIRITUAL JOURNEY

David Gregory

Simon & Schuster Paperbacks

New York   London   Toronto   Sydney   New Delhi

Simon & Schuster Paperbacks
An Imprint of Simon & Schuster, Inc.
1230 Avenue of the Americas
New York, NY 10020

First Simon & Schuster trade paperback edition September 2016

For information about special discounts for bulk purchases, please contact Simon & Schuster Special Sales at 1-866-506-1949 or business@simonandschuster.com

The Simon & Schuster Speakers Bureau can bring authors to your live event. For more information or to book an event contact the Simon & Schuster Speakers Bureau at 1-866-248-3049 or visit our website at www.simonspeakers.com

Interior design by Joy O'Meara

Manufactured in the United States of America

10 9 8 7 6 5 4 3

The Library of Congress has cataloged the hardcover edition as follows:

Gregory, David, 1970–
  How's your faith? : an unlikely spiritual journey / David Gregory. — First Simon & Schuster hardcover edition.
    pages cm.
Includes bibliographical references and index.
ISBN 978-1-4516-5160-7 (hardback) — ISBN 978-1-4516-5161-4 (trade paper) — ISBN 978-1-4516-5162-1 (ebook) 1. Gregory, David, 1970– 2. Spiritual biography. I. Title.
BL73.G735A3 2015
204.092—dc23
  [B]   2015010581

ISBN 978-1-4516-5160-7
ISBN 978-1-4516-5161-4 (pbk)
ISBN 978-1-4516-5162-1(ebook)

For Beth

My inspiration,
My love,
My life

CONTENTS

CONTENTS

KEY FIGURES IN THE BOOK

THE GREGORY FAMILY

Beth Wilkinson—my wife

Don—my father

Carolyn—my mother (Now Carolyn Surtees)

Kaye—my stepmother

Stephanie (nickname Ci)—my sister

RELIGIOUS TEACHERS AND INTERVIEWS

Erica Brown—Jewish educator, author, and my teacher

Rachel Cowan—Rabbi, Jewish educator, author

Michael Cromartie—Vice President, Ethics and Public Policy Center, Washington, D.C.

Cardinal Timothy Dolan—Archbishop of New York

Ginger Gaines-Cirelli—Senior Pastor, Foundry United Methodist Church, Washington, D.C.

KEY FIGURES IN THE BOOK

Larry Hoffman—Rabbi, Professor of Liturgy at Hebrew Union College

Tim Keller—Founding Pastor, Redeemer Presbyterian Church, New York; author

Imam Mohamed Magid—Executive Director, All Dulles Area Muslim Society (ADAMS)

Russell Moore—President, Ethics and Religious Liberty Commission of the Southern Baptist Convention

Joel Osteen—Pastor, Lakewood Church in Houston; author; televangelist

Danny Zemel—Senior Rabbi, Temple Micah, Washington, D.C.

PROLOGUE

The journey to strengthen my faith started a little over ten years ago, when I began feeling a spiritual longing—a desire that stemmed mostly from a sense of deep gratitude: for my life, my marriage, my children, and my career. I realized that I felt vulnerable and that I didn't want to screw it up. I also started wondering what else was expected of me—how I could grow as a person. I wanted to be better.

For most of my life, faith was not part of my vocabulary. For a long time, the big questions in my life were about my career: How could I develop into a credible television journalist? When would I land a network job? Would I have what it took to be an anchor of a major news program? I was young, ambitious, and determined.

The plan came together even better than I'd imagined. I realized many of my goals. But somewhere along the way, I learned that there was more to do. Larger goals to meet.

I was inspired to explore my spirituality more seriously by my wife as we set out to raise a family with strong religious values. When we started thinking about how God would be part of our family life, I realized that I needed to take a deeper look at my own beliefs. And once I started asking myself big questions like "How do you find a sense of meaning and purpose in life?," I concluded that I would find answers only in the search for God.

That's what this book is. It's me turning my journalistic curiosity toward the biggest issues of all: issues like what we're doing here. It's me asking tough questions of some of today's most thoughtful faith leaders—and of myself. Questions like "Who is it that I want to be?" and "How can I best get there?" and "How do I stay on the path even when I fail?" This is far from a religious how-to. Rather, it's an exploration into what's possible through faith, even if I keep falling short.

As my wife, Beth, and I talked about having children, we confronted serious questions about the role of faith in our lives, like many couples do when they start thinking about having kids. Beth grew up religious from a Protestant family. I am a Jew, the product of a Jewish father and a Catholic mother. When Beth pressed me for more depth about my faith, I didn't have a clear answer. "I know what you are," she would say, "but what do you believe?"

The question reverberated. What did I believe? Over time, the answer became crucial to understanding the person I wanted to be and could become. How could I better express gratitude for my good fortune? How could I become more humble and grow as a person, husband, and father? To what could I turn in times of difficulty, with my job or our marriage or the three kids we went on to have?

I wanted to get this right. I wanted my family life to be a deeper experience than my own was, growing up. If we were going to be a Jewish family with a spiritual focus and a higher purpose, I would have to lead. But that meant I had some discovering to do about my faith and myself. I had to find answers to spiritual questions about what I believed about God. And about which, if any, of the Jewish teachings truly resonated with me.

I became a seeker during a momentous time in the world and in my career. I was covering the White House for NBC News during a period of war and highly charged politics. In the terrible days and months after 9/11, I watched President George W. Bush make the decision to involve our country in two wars. Whether his decisions were right or wrong, they were some of the toughest calls a leader can face.

During that time, I had the unusual experience of being asked by President Bush, "How's your faith?" It was startling and memorable to be asked that question by a president of the United States, especially because, as a White House reporter, I was known for asking tough questions of that president and for pushing him hard in press conferences. But President Bush was aware that I'd started down a path of religious exploration. He'd heard about it from a friend who was part of a study group I met with from time to time. And he was curious about it, maybe because it seemed a little unlikely for the person he knew me to be: a TV guy, a politics guy, a little aggressive about my career.

So how was my faith? Well, when forced to think

about it, I had to admit that it was something of an empty page. It's taken a lot of focused energy over almost a dozen years for me to answer the question differently. The query from President Bush reminded me that no matter where you are in life, that question may be the most important one you can be asked.

I've continued to ask it of myself, particularly in the immediate aftermath of losing my job at the helm of *Meet the Press* after twenty years with the network. Parting ways with NBC—and being publicly humiliated in the process—was a great test of my faith. In response, like never before, I sought comfort from God's presence, and found it. As Rabbi Jonathan Sacks, the former chief rabbi of the largest synagogue body in the United Kingdom, once put it: "If you believe in God, you know He pretty well believes in you."

"You must feel like your whole world is crashing down around you," one of my bosses at NBC said to me in the midst of all that. But when I thought about it, that was not how I felt. In fact, I felt solid in myself, my life, my family. My whole world was not crashing down—just my work world.

When I realized I was going to leave NBC, I drove to some woods not far from my house and called my wife. Her support and encouragement helped me get through those moments, but I knew when I hung up the phone that I'd have to rely on my faith in a new way, too.

I pulled over to the side of a quiet street in my neighborhood for a while after I got off the phone, just looking at the trees. I was startled to notice that it wasn't only sadness I was feeling; it was also some peace. It was July, so the trees were full and green. They were white oaks and chestnut oaks that had grown massive over decades. And I thought, Yes, this life event feels huge right now, but in fact it is small. I had this sensation that I was being carried. I felt support and love around me, and I could feel God in that. I thought about what I wanted my kids to learn of hardship, dignity, and grace. I tried to work out how I would tell them that I had lost my job and why that felt so hard. I was thinking about the things that really mattered.

This is a book about my efforts—as a father, as a husband, and as a journalist in the public eye—to understand and deepen my spirituality. It's a story that probes other religions, not just my own, to answer important questions about who we want to be and what we believe. Through my wife, a Protestant, I have come to recognize that my experience is no different from that of many Christians. I am deeply moved by other faiths.

This book follows my journey to find a relationship with God. It's not only about what my own tradition teaches; it's also about lessons I can learn from other faith traditions. It's about becoming the fullest person I can be. Even when I may fail to live up to the expectations of my faith, a spiritual commitment keeps calling me to try again and dig deeper.

Once I got on the bus to take this spiritual journey, I discovered how many people were already on board. I've met extraordinary people of different backgrounds and opinions: people who have shown me the benefit of provoking conversations about faith, especially when we do not all share an answer. I've spent years listening, and I've heard how many of us share this pursuit of meaning and purpose in life.

My search has brought me to the Texas mega-church of the evangelical preacher Joel Osteen, and to the quiet calm of the New York apartment of a female rabbi who converted to Judaism from Christianity. It's taken me back to my mother, a recovering alcoholic in California, who has shown me that life offers you more than one opportunity to redeem yourself. And it's taken me to a Friday-night Shabbat ritual with my Christian wife at home in Washington, D.C.—a ritual that often involves martinis and always involves my kids putting on something other than basketball shorts.

This book has shown me that spiritual journeys are always worth taking, because they transcend the ups and downs of a career or other low moments of life; they are the work of a lifetime. You're not taking a trip if you remain in the same place. I have studied, reflected, debated, sought counsel, and questioned myself, and along the way I have matured spiritually. I have changed, and I am still deeply flawed. The more I try to grow, the more I see how much of a journey is ahead of me.

I hope my own journey will inspire others to look hard at themselves and ask: "How's my faith?"

CHAPTER 1

Pain

The Spiritual Search Begins with the Family Story

———————✳———————

In these pages, I tell secrets about my parents, my children, myself because that is one way of keeping track and because I believe that it is not only more honest but also vastly more interesting than to pretend that I have no such secrets to tell. I not only have my secrets, I am my secrets. And you are your secrets. Our secrets are human secrets, and our trusting each other enough to share them with each other has much to do with the secret of what it is to be human.

—Frederick Buechner, *Listening to Your Life: Daily Meditations with Frederick Buechner*

In a line, this is my spiritual autobiography: I grew up with a strong sense of Jewish identity, but I didn't have much belief.

And it makes sense, given who my parents are. My mom, Carolyn, grew up Catholic and left the faith when my sister and I were still little. She had a bad experience after a stillborn birth in a Catholic hospital, and it turned her against the Catholic Church for good. She was conflicted about whether to baptize us. In the end, my older sister, Stephanie (I called her Ci, pronounced Kigh, because I couldn't pronounce her name) was baptized and I was not; I was named in synagogue. For the most part, Mom was content to leave our religious upbringing to my dad, and Dad's Jewish identity has always been more ethnic than religious.

As a result, I did not think much about God or spirituality. The concepts felt too abstract. My mother encouraged me to pray, in spite of her negative experience with the Church; she told me once at bedtime that speaking to God was as easy as starting a conversation in my head. "Some people might even call Him Champ," she said, knowing that anything to do with the film *Rocky* was likely to inspire me.

I identified with my dad's brand of Jewishness, a cultural identity developed in New York and L.A. I was bar mitzvahed at the Synagogue for the Performing Arts, centered in Beverly Hills. The performing arts part was not a new denomination of our faith but a reflection of where we lived.

My dad, Don, chose the Synagogue for the Performing Arts to celebrate the High Holidays—the times when most Jews attend synagogue—because that was where his community was. It was a warm place with many great families and kids my age. It was also a place that could be easily caricatured, because so many of those who attended were associated with the entertainment industry, and Judaism was commingled with the signs and symbols of Hollywood success.

We held High Holiday services in the headquarters of the Academy of Motion Picture Arts and Sciences in Beverly Hills. Its plush lobby was adorned with photos of Oscar winners and show business figures; for years I thought that the Oscar was a Jewish icon. Inside the theater where services were held, the Greek tragedy and comedy masks adorned the bimah, the elevated platform for the ark containing the Torah.

What stands out in my memory are the older Hollywood figures who came for the High Holidays, the women smelling of perfume and wearing expensive jewelry. There were actors, too. As a kid, I loved that I would sometimes recognize a guy from a commercial I'd seen on TV that week, or even from a well-known movie. People would greet my father, a producer and former agent, from across the room: "A happy and a healthy new year, that's what you should have!"

More than one would comment on how tall I'd gotten since the year before. Members of the congregation were called up to do readings, and this being a congregation of many actors, the readings were memorable. "I'd like to pray," went one. "But I haven't the time. Please, Lord, help us make the time." I remember the comedic actor Red Buttons—a client of my father's—ending a reading once with the line: "Thanks for the club date."

Now I can see how different my childhood faith experience was from that of people who grew up attending church or synagogue every week. Some people might think our synagogue was making a mockery of religion. But that wasn't so at all. It was a serious and warm place, and it gave me a sense of belonging, a sense of comfort and identity. The L.A. part of my Jewish identity, while somewhat funny, was, at its root, not so different from that of many Jews in America. That is to say, identity, Jewish history, and peoplehood were bigger in my upbringing than theology was.

Rabbi David Wolpe, a friend of mine from L.A., once said that Judaism is about two things: family and religion. Family is the shared sense of peoplehood that Jews have; religion is about the texts and the relationship with God. For me, the second part lagged behind. I knew I was Jewish. That's as far as it went. There was no spiritual side to it, no effort to engage with God.

Years later, when I began a spiritual search, I tried to understand what happened in my family when I was growing up and what happened to me. Maybe this is true for all of us. Letting go of what we carry around from childhood is made easier through humility and an emphasis on forgiveness and healing in faith.

I may not have recognized it, but as a kid as young as eleven, my spiritual longing began. I needed something to help me with the most difficult part of my life: my mother's drinking. I had nowhere to go with my feelings about it. I had no sense of community nor was I comfortable turning to those closest to me for help with solving my problems. I also didn't trust that God might carry me through this confusing period. Mom's alcoholism was part of the backdrop of our lives for years, but almost suddenly it took center stage when Mom was arrested for driving drunk in front of me. I was fifteen.

No one asks to be the child of an alcoholic. But you can learn from it, as from any hardship. My mother struggles with her story still, but she has allowed me to share it more widely than ever before here because, she says, owning it and letting others—anyone—learn from it is part of her recovery. Thankfully she did recover. Both of us did.

When I think about how I want my kids' lives to be different from mine, I come up with one simple and small thing: eating meals as a family. That's not something my family did when I was growing up, and I didn't know to miss it. But I'm glad that Beth and I have made an effort to sit us all down together most nights. My memory of meals is of eating Betty Crocker's Hamburger Helper as my mom cleaned up around the kitchen. After my parents split, Mom started working long hours and my sister and I tended to make meals for ourselves at dinnertime.

Even before they divorced, my dad was often not around at mealtimes, because he'd be working late. When he got home, he would play his own made-up hide-and-seek game with my sister and me, based on the old-timey detective radio show *Mr. Keen, Tracer of Lost Persons*. My sister and I would run and hide, pretending Dad was Mike, Mr. Keen's assistant, making a loud call asking Mr. Keen to find two missing children. Though we'd hide under the bed or some other easily discovered place, we couldn't stand the suspense of the game. Dad would keep it going for five minutes or so, using false leads, looking inside closets, and we'd giggle loudly until he finally "found" us.

It's funny how the family meal stands out for me. My memory plays tricks on me. I did have family meals with my dad and stepmom on the weekends after my parents' divorce, and during those years my mom made an effort to have us sit at the table together at least once a week. But as an adult the family meal stands out to me as a symbol of family order. That's what I felt was missing, mostly in my adolescence.

It wasn't a consistently difficult childhood by any means. Still, I lived with a single mom who worked a string of unfulfilling jobs—a mom who gave us as much love as she could through the addiction that had her in its grip—and that experience made me who I am. The hard parts gave me a certain grit. And during those years, a fierce determination grew inside me, a desire to transcend my circumstances. I focused on trying to escape to a career in journalism that would take me far way. I cannot know the objective truth of what happened between my parents when they split up. What matters is that they simply weren't right together. There are indisputable facts: They divorced three and a half years after separating, for example. Dad lived on his own for a time in an apartment in Los Angeles. When Dad remarried, he and my stepmother, Kaye, bought a home off Mulholland Drive, a dividing line between the LA Basin and the San Fernando Valley.

The divorce loomed large over Mom's life for all of my childhood. Even though it was her decision—she had asked my dad to move out—the split marked her as a failure in her own mind. It overshadowed all the little successes in her life. The split was fairly amicable, and my dad says he paid generous child support, but my mom always struggled to make ends meet. She wasn't good with money, as she will admit. She saw herself as a struggling single mom who couldn't possibly match up to him, not only in our eyes but—more to the point—in hers. She saw my dad living a more financially successful life with more career advancement in show business and felt inferior.

From Mom's perspective, she had to remake herself, come up with a new identity, in the years after the divorce. She cycled through a series of different jobs, none of them especially fulfilling: She worked successfully as a Realtor for a while, before she got a job at American Savings Bank. Later, she started selling title insurance, which she liked because it was busy and it got her back out in the world charming people, one of the things she was best at. Her feelings of inadequacy drove her on a downward spiral with drinking. My mom loved having us for the majority of the week, but she struggled with the idea that all our "fun time" was reserved for weekends with Dad. This was the story she was telling herself: that the fun times we did enjoy with Dad somehow tipped the balance—that we would come to favor him over her. The truth is we enjoyed good times with both.

My mom's drinking frayed her around the edges, but she still functioned. She was a memorable person, and she knew it—ready with a big laugh and a sometimes outrageous sense of humor. She told me that the drinking, before it reached a problem stage, helped her turn on the charm and overcome nervousness or insecurity. Mom was just five-five, with the physical confidence of the dancer she once was. Her frosted blond hair was often teased up a little with hair spray. She dressed in a casual California style, favoring loose outfits in bold patterns with chunky jewelry. She had a smile that made people want to smile back. She might talk in an exaggerated New York accent to be silly, as though she were a Jewish mother from the Upper West Side rather than a Catholic girl from Burbank.

Mom was always dedicated to us, even during the worst of her drinking. She took Ci and me on trips to Catalina Island with her friends, and out to eat at an Italian place called Mike's for sausage pizza after my Little League games. Ci and I often got two Thanksgivings: one with our dad and Kaye, then a second with our mom, who sometimes rented a condo in Palm Springs, where we'd watch the Cowboys play on TV.

When money got tight, Mom would buy things for us on layaway. She found a way to get me a Commodore computer when I was eleven, because I asked for it, though it was more than she could afford; she wanted to support me. There was no doubt that we were loved. However, her addiction made her unreliable and inconsistent. By the time I was in high school, the drinking had become a regular part of our lives. While she was in control for many years, the bad moments stand out and dominate my memories of my adolescence.

Such as a spring Saturday in 1986. Mom was forty-five, and she'd been a single mother of two for almost a decade. I was a sophomore at Birmingham High School, a public school in the San Fernando Valley, and I was already tall, in the lanky and awkward way of teenage boys. That morning she drove me to school for a tournament with the Speech and Debate Club. I'd joined earlier that year, and I got a lot of encouragement from the coach, Ann Collins, a strong-willed woman of high standards.

My mom had no idea how much I loved the Speech and Debate Club. It was so different from my home life. Everything Mrs. Collins did seemed understated, controlled: quite a contrast to my mom, whose outsize personality always took center stage. Mrs. Collins wore her white hair in a short, conservative cut; I remember her in fitted polyester slacks and a pair of glasses whose tint would darken when she stepped outside—and sometimes when she was inside.

I appreciated Mrs. Collins's strict rules about public speaking and thrived under her discipline. The only time she wasn't formal and guarded was when she was dispensing advice. "Stand up straight," she would tell me in a singsong voice. She had a lyrical way of speaking, and she'd adopt the correct posture to demonstrate. "Project to the back of the room," she'd say.

After I started winning debates, Mrs. Collins gave me a suggestion I never forgot: "You'll always need someone around to remind you that you aren't as good as you think you are." Little did she know I'd be lucky enough to be surrounded by many such people once I was in the public eye.

Mrs. Collins had urged me to participate in the Saturday tournament at my school. It was an all-day affair, with participants from schools all over the city. At the end of the day, I qualified for the state competition in two events. It was a great feeling. I'd never won at anything.

It was early evening by the time it was all finished, and I called my mom from the pay phone bank to ask her to come pick me up. As soon as I said, "It's me, Mom," she started crying. Clearly, she had been drinking—she was slurring her words and her voice was louder, the way she got after a few glasses of wine. "I didn't know where you were," she said, and I spoke slowly and clearly when I replied, "But you did know where I was. I'm at the tournament. I've been here all day."

When I told her that I'd won and was going to the state competition, she cried some more. I felt uncomfortable at the phone bank, even though there was no one around to overhear. I waited until she'd calmed down and then asked her to come pick me up, which she did. We lived within five minutes of my school. When I got in the car, she hugged me and said, "This is so great. We have to go celebrate." It never occurred to me that it would be dangerous getting in the car with her. I didn't think about risk like that. I was used to being with her like this.

We drove to Anna's in Sherman Oaks, my mom's favorite restaurant and bar. It was one of these dimly lit Italian places with red velvet booths in the restaurant area and a large bar in the back, which was where the hard-core drinkers clustered. Anna's filled up with professionals during weekday lunch hours and evenings; many of them were heavy drinkers, like Mom. Since Anna's was in the building where my mom worked as an investment officer at American Savings Bank, I am confident that she spent a lot of time there.

Mom started early and continued through the evening. But even during the worst of her drinking, Mom rarely spent more than a couple of hours at Anna's each night. She'd always come home around dinnertime. Even though we weren't all sitting down for dinner together, and even if she was drunk, she felt it was important to be available to us in some way.

Mom knew all the bartenders at Anna's, and she was special buddies with a guy named Stan, who favored polyester pants and plenty of hair spray on his comb-over. He looked, as Ci once said, like a cruise ship bartender. In high school, Ci started working at Anna's as a cashier on the weekends, as a way of keeping an eye on Mom. She felt responsible for Mom in a way I didn't. Ci was the caretaker and enabler of the family—that's how she puts it now that she's worked through our childhood and is licensed as a therapist. I played a different role in our family dynamic. When things got bad with Mom, I got angry and retreated.

That night Mom and I sat at a booth at Anna's. I had chicken Parmesan and a Coke while Mom put away a few Big Reds, the drink that Stan had named for her: a goblet-sized glass of Chianti filled to the top. A doctor once made the mistake of telling my mom that red wine was the best thing to drink if she was going to. "So I took that as permission," she told me later. "I remember think-ing: Great. The goblet's mine."

I felt uneasy that evening, with one eye on the wine Mom was putting away. The low-level stress of trying to manage her was a familiar feeling. Mom says she never kept track of how many glasses she drank, that alcoholics never do. But Ci and I kept count when we were with her, and Ci often told her she'd had enough.

I imagine Mom was fairly drunk by the time we left Anna's, since she'd gotten started before she came to get me. She was swerving all over Interstate 405 in her brown Mazda 626. "You're not staying straight, Mom," I said. And then, getting more concerned: "Hey—why don't I steer?" I knew I needed to take control of the sit-uation, so I steered from the passenger seat.

I don't remember Mom arguing with me; I didn't think much about it at the time. I just did what I needed to do to get us home. Now I am amazed that Mom and I didn't talk about it afterward. I wish I'd had the where-withal to say, "What was going on there, Mom?" and tell her she was out of control. But as a kid, you don't get to live everybody else's life. Your own normal is all you know.

Mom was born in Detroit. Her parents divorced when she was just four. That was unusual enough among Irish Catholics at the time, but perhaps more unusual was that my grandmother later remarried—and outside her com-munity, to a Protestant. This was not an era of interfaith marriages in any community. Most Americans, especially immigrant Americans, lived in relatively homogeneous religious communities. But my grandmother was a fierce and formidable woman, to put it nicely. She was well equipped to deal with her community's disapproval.

However, she felt strongly the affinity to Catholicism. In an effort to compensate, she insisted that her daughter be brought up strictly Catholic. My mom attended parochial schools and went to church every Sunday, like everyone she knew.

My grandmother's second husband was a navy man. After they married, they moved to Burbank, California, where they found a modest two-bedroom postwar house in a military-subsidized neighborhood. Their new community was not religious or ethnic. Their neighbors were fellow servicemen returned from World War II. My grandmother worked as a switchboard operator at the Burbank airport, and her husband worked as an appliance mechanic.

My biological grandfather had died of cirrhosis of the liver in Detroit when my mom was fourteen. His side of the family was a long line of alcoholics. In true Irish tradition, there are some great stories of booze, misery, and murder in the family lore. His sister, my mom's aunt, fell down the stairs after one big night of drinking. Her father put her to bed, and when she didn't come down for breakfast the next morning, they went up to find her dead. My mom's uncle was shot dead by his wife after he came home drunk and abused her one too many times. There are lots of cheery Irish tales like that from the immigrant community in Detroit.

My mother's passion, from a young age, was show business, as it was for so many girls growing up in Southern California. As a kid, she took dance lessons four times a week, and after she finished high school, she left home to start performing with lounge acts in Las Vegas and Tahoe: leg kicks in sequined leotards, that kind of thing. Mom didn't go to college; she says show business was her education.

Above all, what Mom wanted was to have children. So on her first ever visit to New York, when she fell for a smart and charming agent seven years older than she was, she decided she wanted to make a life with him. Don Gregory did not hide that he was Jewish, by any means, although he had changed his name from Ginsberg to Gregory, since an ethnically recognizable name was considered a disadvantage in the entertainment industry of the 1950s.

To my mom, Don Gregory was "just very New York," as she puts it, meaning that he seemed representative of a cultural identity she knew from movies and books. He was a big guy with a dynamic personality who was not afraid to be aggressive in his career. His showy connections and sharp wit could make my mom feel somewhat provincial.

But Dad also made my mother feel important. They were married when she was twenty-three, with the understanding that she would quit show business. In theory, my mom was fine with that decision, though it was hard for her. My father says that she couldn't stand feeling as though her identity had been subsumed into his, that she was now "just" Mrs. Don Gregory. She always identified with show business—she still does, even though she hasn't danced professionally in fifty years.

My mom also identified as a drinker, as only serious drinkers do. The story of her very first drink is engraved on her memory; she told it to Ci and me when we were little. She was fourteen, and her parents were having a big barbecue for their anniversary. Everyone was out on the back patio, and she sneaked into the kitchen, picked up a bottle of gin—she doesn't remember the brand, but it was a frosted bottle—and took a swig.

"I thought I was going to die," she told me. "My whole mouth went on fire. Then I had another one and got instantly drunk." She found a sofa somewhere and blacked out.

It's impossible to judge how much my mom's drinking contributed to her other difficulties in life: Did they stem from her alcoholism or vice versa? Before the divorce, my dad occasionally complained to Mom about the fact that "she couldn't hold her liquor," as he put it. He says she sometimes slurred her words or acted in a dramatic, embarrassing way when they were out with friends. This would lead to arguments, though neither of them considers Mom's drinking the biggest factor in the collapse of their marriage.

"When a marriage goes bad, there's lots of ways you can describe it" is how my father put it recently, with the perspective of almost forty years between him and his divorce. "And there are lots of things you can blame it on. Drinking was just one of them."

My mother's most serious relationship after the divorce was with Ron, who lived with us for most of the five years they were together. He worked overnights in the film industry, doing color processing, so he was often home when Ci and I got back from school. In spite of his strange schedule, he made our little family seem more complete. He'd play ball with me out in the front yard, or tennis at a nearby park, and I'd sit with him as he watched afternoon reruns of *Hawaii Five-0* before heading off to work.

In 1986 their relationship unraveled and he moved out. Ci and I were upset. His presence in our house had grounded Mom. Sure enough, she doubled down on the drinking after the breakup. That year, my sophomore year of high school, she began to seriously decline. There was always a box of red wine in the fridge, and she sometimes took a glass with her up to bed. She and some friends from our townhouse complex would spend hours soaking in the hot tub, drinking plastic cups of vodka and grapefruit juice. Taken together there was routine to her drinking that extended well beyond cocktail hour. We didn't know it at the time, but she even started to drink vodka in the morning.

When I spent time with my sister recently, we realized that we had very different experiences of the extent of our mom's drinking problem. The twenty-two months between us seemed like a lot in high school. During the worst years of our mom's drinking, Ci was more independent than I was. She already had her driver's license; she wasn't reliant on Mom for rides. She had a serious boyfriend, so she was home less than I was. She didn't witness as much as I did.

One of my memories that Ci didn't share is seeing Mom hit an emotional low point one evening after work. She was crying about Ron when she got home one night, and her crying degenerated into a screaming fit. Not knowing what else to do, I physically restrained her on the floor next to her bed. As I held her down, I caught sight of myself in the floor-to-ceiling mirror. She was still dressed from the office in a black leather business suit. I remember thinking resentfully: This is not the experience a fifteen-year-old should be having. I didn't like being dragged into my mother's emotional life. I was an adolescent boy ill equipped for this reality show.

I never considered telling anyone other than Ci about that terrible moment with Mom. When you are the child of an alcoholic, you instinctively understand how ashamed you would be if the secret became public. No one had to tell me to hold the secret close; that went without saying. Ci and I were engaged in a total cover-up about the extent of our mother's drinking. It was our unspoken pact. We were in it together.

Back when I was as young as five or six, Ci and I conspired to confront Mom about her drinking. I have just a vague memory of what happened, but we found Mom drinking wine while sitting at the kitchen table one afternoon. We stood in front of her, and Ci said with all the moral judgment an oldest child can muster: "You should stop talking on the phone and drinking wine when we get home from school."

It's easy to picture my mother as a drunk throughout my childhood. But it wasn't like that. Mom was a drinker the way many were. She says now, "I took the drink, but eventually the drink took me." Hers was a more jagged path. Drinking was always there, but only captured her fully when her life unraveled.

Once, my best friend in high school, Corey, took the jug of vodka down from the top of the fridge where Mom kept it, and he pretended to swig from the bottle. He acted drunk, stumbling around. I laughed with him while he goofed around, but after that, I was even less likely to confide in him about the real-life vodka drama at home. Years later, I felt angry with Corey and my other high school friends for not probing more. I wished they'd known something was wrong, that they'd asked me what was going on. When I asked Corey about it in adulthood, he said he didn't know about my mom's alcoholism until everyone found out, and he and I didn't talk about it until we were both in college. By then I was talking about Mom a lot more; it wasn't the fraught topic that it was for me in high school. By college my mother was deeper into sobriety and I was getting over my anger enough to get closer to her once again. In high school, I didn't talk about it. No one knew, because I refused to let anyone in. I kept secrets from my friends and in some ways from myself. It was as though I thought that if I didn't talk or think about it, perhaps I could pretend it hadn't happened, hadn't affected me.

Ci and I never told Dad, either, because as bad as things got with Mom, neither of us wanted to live with him—especially not Ci, whose close relationship to our mom created some strain between her and our dad. That said, our relationship with Dad improved after the divorce, when we would have concentrated stints of time with him alone. In the first years after Dad met Kaye, she worked as a flight attendant, so she wasn't around much on the weekends. Ci and I had to establish a relationship with Dad, and while we were initially reluctant, we warmed up.

The three of us developed a Friday-night ritual at this little greasy restaurant called Ready GO on Sunset Boulevard, with booths and bad lighting, where I'd order grape soda. Later, we would all gather on a pullout couch in the den of Dad's apartment (where he lived before he and Kaye bought their house) and watch *The Love Boat*. These are great memories. Still, we never had the ease with Dad that we had with Mom. We'd always been afraid of his temper. He had a big voice and a full dark beard that added to the fearsome impression. Dad could be alternately charming and intimidating. We'd seen him have outbursts—not only at us but at people he worked with. As much as things improved, we always felt as though we had to present to him and Kaye as perfect children. We didn't feel free to be ourselves. If Ci and I were fighting, we'd stop when we heard him coming down the hall.

I remember asking for my sister's help to be sure I didn't forget to bring something to Dad's as I packed my hard black suitcase at Mom's house. We didn't keep a set of clothes and toys at his house, and if we forgot something—such as colored socks for me to wear when we went out to dinner, that was a big one—Dad would get mad.

But he was determined to give us a good time, and Kaye was loving and fun. I immediately developed a strong bond with her, and that made it easier. They would fill our weekends with activities. We'd go to Dodgers games practically every weekend they were in town. Kaye hung a large poster of Steve Garvey over my bed, which endeared her to me. (I was obsessed with Steve Garvey, as she well knew.) During my senior year of high school, in spite of my loyalty to my mom, I moved in with my dad and Kaye. By that point, I felt more comfortable with them and my relationship with my mother was strained.

There's a part of me that wishes I'd done so earlier. I wonder whether my fifteen-year-old self shouldn't have said to my mom: "Look, Mom, you're out of control. I'm going to live with Dad." But that was never going to happen. Ci and I were fiercely protective of Mom. Kaye remembers Ci grabbing my hand and digging her fingernails into my palm if I said something she thought was too revealing about Mom or our home life. We didn't want to give away Mom's secrets, not even to our father.

It was only with each other that Ci and I could be honest during the worst of Mom's drinking. When I could hear Mom talking loudly and drunkenly on the phone downstairs, I'd knock on Ci's door and go into her room through the connecting corridor. I remember sitting on

Ci's bed, twisting the top off of a big brass bedpost that didn't fit quite right. I'd roll the top around in my hands as we discussed Mom's latest incident, like the time she told us she got a bruise on her nose from tripping over the dog. Ci and I both knew she'd fallen while she was drunk, and getting confirmation from each other made us feel better. Nothing terrible ever happened—Mom was never grievously injured—but the potential was always there.

We were in denial about dealing with our anxiety, though. And the denial spilled over into other aspects of my life. For example, I refused to deal with the acne I suffered from as a teenager. When a dermatologist recommended I take Accutane to clear it up, I refused. My dad remembers me yelling at him angrily for daring to make the reasonable suggestion that I follow the dermatologist's advice. If Ci said something about the acne as we washed our faces in the bathroom, I would dismiss it with a joke. "It's just civil unrest," I'd say, as if dispassionately describing the anti-apartheid movement a world away in South Africa. She'd laugh, and that would be the end of it. Inside, I felt terrible about my skin. But I was shut down about it. My appearance was out of my control, like much of my life. I was incapable of mustering the will to deal with it.

My sister and I each developed strategies to navigate Mom's addiction. There was a rhythm to her drinking, a regularity to its patterns when it was at its worst. The best time to talk to her was in the morning, when she was lucid and calm. I always asked for my lunch money before school—a dollar and a quarter—and that was my moment to convey anything else I needed to tell her. I could count on her then.

I knew to stay out of Mom's way when she was drunk and emotional, which was many evenings of the week, after she got home from work and Anna's. She'd stand in the kitchen, talking on the phone to her girlfriends, drinking red wine, and biting her nails. To this day, when I see people biting their nails, it makes me think of the nervousness Mom displayed while drinking.

At night, she was likely to be belligerent with me about the annoying teenage-boy things I did: losing my keys, refusing to pick up my room. We fought a lot. Sometimes she'd threaten to call my dad and would scribble notes to herself about what she wanted to tell him. Her chicken scrawl would have made her level of intoxication apparent to anyone who'd looked at it—not that I needed further confirmation.

From my mom's perspective, things were not too far from normal. As she put it many years later, "I might have functioned blurry, but I functioned. Bills were paid. Cars were running. Children were in school. But what happens when you reach your bottom is slowly but surely, you unravel. And I was unraveling." When I've talked about this period with her, she's told me that she was trying to numb herself. "I was scared. Scared of losing you guys to your father. Of losing my ability to find a mate. Of losing my ability to make money."

My sense of being disconnected from what I was feeling, and of having no control over my home life, made me retreat into my room and do my own thing. I'd spend hours sitting at the TV tray that I used as a desk, focusing on my homework and my debate efforts. I'd listen to baseball games on the radio while I worked, and that always made me happy.

And I'd turn on the nightly news. Come the end of my sophomore year, I'd set my sights on becoming a TV journalist. I realize now that the trials at home gave me a real gift. I could escape my secrets by imagining myself as an authoritative and curious journalist. I might have done something self-destructive with the emptiness I felt during those years, but I was never compelled in that direction, even though I knew guys who were taking drugs and driving fast cars. I channeled my unhappiness into my ambition. It was just where I naturally turned. My goals propelled and centered me. They became what I had to look forward to in the world.

It was then that I started having intense talks with my dad about my future. Once he saw I was determined to go into journalism, he encouraged me like no one else. He especially understood my interest in TV journalism: It was close enough to the entertainment industry that he felt he could offer some useful advice. There were topics I did not want to broach with him at all—such as Mom's drinking or girls I liked—but when it came to the biggest focus in my life, he was a pillar for me. His interest in my career ambitions made me feel loved and attended to.

My dad had always involved me in his career. For a while, I wanted nothing more than to go into show business, too. Dad likes to tell a story of finding me sitting at his desk when I was seven or eight, conducting a mock phone call in which I was pretending to negotiate a deal.

He used to bring Ci and me to New York to see his shows. To this day, when I smell the scent of hot pretzels on the street in Manhattan, I get a visceral memory of my dad striding quickly up Fifth Avenue in the winter with me rushing alongside him, trying to keep up. He and Kaye would bring freshly squeezed orange juice and powdered doughnuts to the midtown hotel where Ci and I would stay in a room adjoining theirs. We loved it. I remember going with Dad to lunches with directors and actors. He took Ci and me to the theater all the time. We would go out with him afterward, late, to Sardi's or Joe Allen, the big restaurants in the theater district.

Those trips enamored me of New York. I wanted the city to be the theme for my bar mitzvah party. I strutted into my party to the Frank Sinatra song "New York, New York"; my cake had the city skyline on it. In the picture taken that morning, I am posing at the foot of our townhouse stairs, wearing a white dinner jacket and a red bow tie, which I believed conveyed the image of the cosmopolitan guy I aspired to be.

The gift that my dad gave me was dreaming with me. He helped me nurture my dreams and formulate them into an actual, realistic path. We talked about my plans for my future almost every weekend that I spent with him during my high school years. I remember staying up on Saturday nights after we got home from dinner or the movies with my stepmother and sister. He would change out of his work clothes and put on his big blue bathrobe, and we'd sit together in the living room. It was a formal room, with high ceilings, elegant couches, a big painting, and a mirror. Dad usually made a point of asking what I'd been thinking about that week, so he could help me with it. He'd give me ideas on how to construct my college essay, and then we'd imagine how I could get ahead once I was working inside a media organization.

Looking back, I realize how many hours Dad and I spent discussing what I would *become* and how little time on who I *was*. It was as if Dad knew my life with Mom was a secret I needed to keep from him and everyone else; as if he knew that a career in TV journalism would permit me to create a David Gregory who had a perfect life, perfect hair, and perhaps even perfect skin.

I decided on journalism early in high school, as I watched the nightly news on the tiny TV in my bedroom. With the lights out and the house quiet around me, some reporters could make me feel as though I were in the middle of a war zone in the Middle East or tackling a tornado in the Midwest. I loved imagining myself grappling with the story, getting a handle on the history of it, and translating it for audiences back at home.

During high school, I studied the morning and evening news shows, trying to work out why different reporters and anchors did what they did. I memorized writing and narration patterns. I'd even mimic those I most admired, Tom Brokaw and Peter Jennings. I was moved by the coverage of the nuclear accident at Chernobyl and the *Challenger* disaster. The following year, I was riveted by the Iran-Contra hearings. I didn't understand all the issues at play, but I locked in to the testimony of Oliver North. I followed it like a daily sporting event, almost as obsessively as I checked Steve Garvey's box score each morning in the newspaper.

April 24, 1986. It's a date with great significance. It marks an all-time low for my mother but also a birth.

When the day began, its only significance was that I was competing in a statewide speaking tournament sponsored by Optimist International. I was to give a speech about the importance of optimism. The speech was supposed to address the importance of a positive attitude. Now this strikes me as somewhat ironic. It's hard to imagine myself brimming with optimism at that stage in my life.

The competition was in Agoura Hills, and I rode with Mrs. Collins, the debate coach, and a couple of other kids who were competing. Mom planned to come later to watch me. After she arrived, I caught sight of her from the podium. She was sitting next to Heidi, one of her drinking buddies from work. Mom was already crying, and I don't think I'd even started speaking yet. That was a sure sign she was drunk. Later, she told me she and Heidi had stopped by a party on the way to the competition, but she insisted that because she'd had a sandwich, she couldn't have been too inebriated.

To my surprise, I won in my category. I must have somehow delivered my remarks on optimism with conviction. Mom clapped loudly and rushed up to me. While I often recoiled from my mom's oversize emotions, I was used to them. I was proud of myself, too. I hugged her back and tried to tamp down her emotion and head out to the car. Now I understand that my small successes in high school probably made Mom feel better about herself. My winning a competition might have made it easier for her to justify her drinking: She could tell herself that her kids were clearly doing fine.

I no longer recall the logistics, but Mrs. Collins needed a ride home with us. We all climbed into Mom's Mazda—Mom driving, Heidi in the passenger seat, and Mrs. Collins in the backseat with me. I had become fairly accustomed to driving with Mom tipsy. But this evening it was more noticeable than usual. She was driving like she had the time after Anna's when I grabbed the steering wheel, weaving unreliably between lanes on the freeway. I was especially unnerved by it because I was sitting next to a respected mentor whose approval I sought. Mrs. Collins looked uneasy, and that only worsened my discomfort. She sat up straight and drew her breath in sharply as Mom swerved.

It wasn't long before a highway patrolman's lights began flashing behind us. When I saw the blue lights hit the car, my head began to pound. Mom is getting pulled over, I thought, and I panicked about what would happen next. She got out of the car and we heard her talking. Her voice sounded loud and argumentative to me. I remember Mrs. Collins saying pointedly—as if offering me a school lesson—"This is a time when you *don't* want to say much." Unfortunately, Mom couldn't hear her. Something tells me she wouldn't have been quite in the place to accept advice from my debate coach, anyway.

The officer asked Mom to do the "walk and turn" test alongside the car to check her sobriety. When she failed the test, she asked him not to handcuff her in front of the car and me. She walked back over to the car and leaned into the window toward me. There was no sense of reckoning in her face, no sorrow in her eyes—just the same old dodge. Everything would be okay, she told me; the officer was doing this only because he was inexperienced. He walked her away, handcuffed her, and put her in his patrol car.

I was worried for Mom, going off to some jail somewhere. But I have to admit that my bigger focus was more self-involved. I felt a deep sense of embarrassment. This was a new low. This night represented my utter failure to shield our life from outsiders. I tried to avoid Mrs. Collins's eye. But the secret was out.

Mrs. Collins volunteered to drive Heidi and me home in my mother's Mazda. It was a quiet car ride. I don't think I spoke at all. In fact, I remember little about that night after seeing Mom get in the back of the police car.

The house was dark when I got back. Ci was in bed. She'd been trying to sleep but had been wondering where we were. I walked into the dark of her room and announced: "Mom got arrested tonight." Ci told me later that my voice was angry. She asked lots of questions—where

Mom was and how long she'd be in jail—but I went silent. These were questions I didn't know the answers to. We discussed whether we would call Dad and decided not to. That was it. I went to my room and went to bed.

Mom spent the night on a cot in a shared cell in the Calabasas jail, waiting for Ron to pick her up after he finished his shift that night. Although they'd split up, they were still close and she could rely on him to be caring, so he was the natural person for her to call. Mom used her pay phone access to call my sister collect all night long. I didn't hear the phone—my sister had her own line in her room—and I was shocked when Ci told me Mom had kept her up all night. Ci didn't mind. "Mom was just trying to get through it," she told me later. "And she was getting through it with me, which is who she got through things with at the time." In many ways, Ci was more like a girlfriend than a daughter to Mom.

Waking up the next morning in jail, Mom says she felt a small measure of relief, akin to the sensation a criminal might feel when she's tired of running and ready to make it end. Overpowering that emotion, though, were shame and fear.

"The first thing I thought was: My life is over," Mom told me later. "Meaning I could never get past this. I couldn't ever fix it."

Mom's arrest was a terrible blow for Dad, too. Here was irrefutable evidence that he was in the dark about a major part of our lives.

Dad later told me that he and Kaye stayed up most of the night after they heard that Mom was in jail, talking about whether they should have us come and live with them. It had to be a real wake-up moment for my father. My own view is that he had never admitted to himself that Mom had a real problem with alcohol.

As an adult, I've wondered how my dad and others close to us didn't notice that something was off. But it was harder in those days to recognize someone as an alcoholic, let alone call him or her out. Alcoholism wasn't yet a national concern. Public awareness of substance abuse, and its impact on children, was much lower in the 1970s and '80s. It was also the pre-*Oprah* era, a more private time, at the tail end of the 1950s mentality that assumed outsiders were not to intrude on the nuclear family. "Danger has degrees," my dad said recently when I pressed him about whether it was unsafe for us to be living with Mom.

Still, I spent several years being angry at Dad for failing to remove us from the situation. I felt that he should have known better than to leave Ci and me with Mom when she was in such a bad way. Now I'm not so sure. Even after Mom was arrested, Dad says, he felt it would do more harm than good to try to get full custody. It would have meant going to court, putting us on the stand. He wasn't willing to expose us to that.

The morning after Mom's arrest is mostly a blank for me. She wasn't home when I went to school, and I don't remember seeing Ci, either. Once I got to school, I went to see Mrs. Collins and told her I was sorry. She looked at me solemnly from across her desk. "You know you don't need to apologize," she said. "You do not need to say that. Your mom needs you right now." I thanked her and backed away to go to class.

I've wondered about that conversation in the years since. Why didn't Mrs. Collins ask me more about how I was doing that morning? Sure, my mom needed me, but I needed help, too. I imagine that Mrs. Collins was reluctant to intervene in my life, though.

My mom's arrest began a long thawing process. It took months, but gradually, I began to let go of my secrets. Little by little, I began to feel more comfortable with putting myself out there. The biggest change stemmed from Mom and the enormous transformation she was about to go through.

When I got home from school that day, Mom was standing in a corner of the little living room of our townhouse, not a place we would normally congregate. Everything felt strange and slightly out of place. Ron was looming behind her protectively on the stairs. Later, I found out he'd helped Mom get rid of all the alcohol in the house that day.

Mom looked like a wreck, as though she'd been crying for days. She held out a hand to me and said, "I am so sorry, Davey."

I didn't want to look at her. I just mumbled, "It's okay, it's fine."

She said, "No, it's not okay. It's absolutely not okay." And then she told me she was going to get help. She was going to a recovery program meeting that evening.

I don't remember feeling relief, or happiness, or pride, or any of the things I wish I'd been able to feel in that moment. I remember only a dull familiar anger. I had been worried about her over the last year or so, as she had taken a precipitous decline. Managing her had been stressful. I had become accustomed to numbing myself emotionally when she was drinking. Now that she had embarrassed herself to such an extreme, I just wanted to back away.

In Mary Karr's book *Lit: A Memoir,* about her own descent into alcoholism, she wrote that her young son was the reason she knew she had to survive. "You were the agent of my rescue," she wrote of him. "Not a good job for someone barely three feet tall."

There's no doubt that Mom went to the meeting that night not because she got a DUI but because her son had witnessed her being handcuffed and driven off to jail in a police car. I was never particularly comfortable being the catalyst for Mom to try to get sober. For many years, I considered her a huge burden. But she was my mother, and I loved her. At some point I realized how lucky I was that she wanted to change her life.

CHAPTER 2

Love

Good Things Can Emerge from Tragedy

---✳---

I fell in love with a woman seeking the death penalty for a notorious terrorist. She ultimately changed the way I think about faith and God.

But first, the news.

It was early 1997, and I'd been assigned to cover the trial of Oklahoma City bomber Timothy McVeigh. In our post-9/11 world, it's easy to lose sight of the gravity of the Oklahoma City bombing and the trial that followed. But when Gulf War army veteran Timothy McVeigh detonated a truck bomb outside a federal building in Oklahoma City, it was an unprecedented act of terror in the heartland of the country. He killed 168 people on April 19, 1995, including 19 children, and injured more than 500, making it the deadliest terrorist attack on American soil until September 11, 2001. It shocked and frightened the American public like nothing before.

The trial was a major news event, especially in the wake of the not-guilty verdict in the criminal trial of O. J. Simpson. Fearing a fair trial was not possible in Oklahoma, the 10th Circuit had transferred the case to Judge Richard Matsch, a U.S. District Court judge in Denver. I followed the case there, having just finished up a reporting stint in Los Angeles on O.J.'s civil trial, which continued through early 1997.

Millions of Americans tuned in to watch the 133 days of televised courtroom testimony in the Simpson criminal case, and a stunning 150 million people watched the verdict, making it one of the most watched events in television history. Dubbed the "trial of the century," it conditioned the media to cover other high-profile cases.

From the start, the McVeigh trial was imbued with greater gravity, starting with the fact that no cameras were allowed in the courtroom. The Oklahoma City trial was a moment of reckoning for America: Two U.S. citizens had masterminded a terrorist attack that hit in the heartland and destroyed thousands of lives. It was clear that McVeigh's would be more than a show trial. There had been no federal executions since 1963, but the government was going to pursue the death penalty.

Timothy McVeigh had said he was enraged by the government's 1993 siege of the Branch Davidian compound near Waco, Texas. The Waco siege, which began when the federal government attempted to seize weapons from the home of an apocalyptic Christian sect,

lasted over seven weeks and resulted
deaths, a mass suicide by cult members w
pound was breached. Conducted by federal
the siege was widely criticized. That very night, A
General Janet Reno called her government's plan to
sault the heavily armed compound "a mistake."

While many Americans were deeply troubled by the deaths resulting from the Waco siege, McVeigh's anger stemmed from a different source: his fervent opposition to the seizure of the weapons. Like other far-right activists at the time, he'd been enraged by the Brady gun control bill—the 1993 law requiring background checks on handgun purchases. It's interesting to recall this now, since the issue of restricting access to guns has not retreated from today's political discourse.

It emerged during the trial that McVeigh had paid a visit to the Waco compound when it was under siege. He told a guy at a gun show that he'd crawled under the fence and back out, without being seen by the federal agents patrolling the perimeter. As revealed in a picture in a student newspaper that was introduced at trial, McVeigh sat on his car selling anti-government bumper stickers to protest the ATF. The prosecution team would argue that McVeigh targeted the federal building in Oklahoma City because several ATF agents were among those who worked there.

It's a measure of the importance of the McVeigh trial that NBC had assigned four correspondents to cover it full-time, all the way from jury selection in early 1997 through the guilty verdict that June. As horrific as the

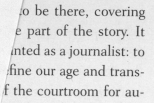

to be there, covering
e part of the story. It
nted as a journalist: to
fine our age and trans-
f the courtroom for au-

like some kind of payoff
n. It was a major assign-
ior reporter on the story. I
was just t.   een hired by NBC the year
before—a full four years before I'd expected to make
it to a network. It seemed my father's late-night career
talks had helped. "Never let anyone else say no for you"
was one of my dad's stock phrases. He'd learned as an
agent that it was worth it to make a call instead of as-
suming that something wouldn't happen. "Always keep
your goals in front of you," he'd say.

When I was at American University, I spent more
time thinking about my career than about anything else.
Unlike kids who use their college years to figure out what
they like or what they're good at, I already knew—or at
least I thought I did. Although I was interested in my
college major, international affairs, I couldn't relax into
college life. I was impatient: actively seeking internships,
working long hours as the news director at the university
TV station, and setting up a stringing gig with an ABC
affiliate station in Tucson, Arizona.

When I was twenty-three and working for the CBS
affiliate in Albuquerque, I would lie awake in bed at
night, imagining the life of a network news correspon-

dent. I wanted to experience the world the way the older generation of photographers and reporters had, chronicling wars and revolutions. The work was fascinating and important, and the life sounded romantic: hustling and rushing, all in the hope of being one of Tom Brokaw's guys. To me, nothing sounded better than reporting big stories for the nightly news. The more I was on TV, the more I wanted to be on TV.

Since graduating, I'd lived in Albuquerque, Sacramento, L.A., and Chicago for different jobs. As exciting as the travel and the news were, I spent my hours daydreaming about making a jump to a bigger market. To that end, I would write letters to the correspondents I most admired, such as Bernie Goldberg of CBS, who wrote back that he was going to plaster my adoring note on the side of the Empire State Building.

In Albuquerque, I met Scott Pelley, a Dallas-based correspondent for CBS News who was becoming a big deal; he went on to become anchor of the *CBS Evening News* and a correspondent for *60 Minutes.* I'd taken note of every career move Pelley had made, constantly measuring his path against the one I was trying to cut for myself.

Pelley came to Albuquerque to cover a story I'd been working on for a year, about the sexual abuse of boys inside the Catholic Church. Since I was working for the local CBS affiliate, I promised to give his producer all of my tapes and contacts, with one condition: that I could meet with Scott to learn all about his career. When the meeting happened, I was thrilled. I asked if he'd like to see a tape I'd compiled of some of his work. He declined politely, and I realized my behavior made me seem like something of a stalker.

When I was assigned to cover McVeigh, I was just starting to break through on *Today* and cable news shows. I hadn't cracked Brokaw's *Nightly News* yet. But I was on my way, and I had the headstrong, cocky assurance of a guy who knew it. Airports, last-minute plans, the rush of that first moment arriving into a new story: That was the life I wanted, roaming alone from story to story, without commitments.

Everything was subservient to my career. My love interests had always been pretty fleeting. I stayed away from anything long-term, not wanting the complications. I never had a chance to long for partnership, though I felt lonely and isolated sometimes, roving from city to city. I certainly did not make time for any sort of spiritual life or to reflect upon what was important to me beyond my career. All of this is to say that when Beth Wilkinson came into my life, I wasn't looking for anything. She changed that.

Beth was a rising star at the Justice Department, and she'd come to Denver as one of four main prosecutors on the team representing the U.S. government in the case against Timothy McVeigh. I encountered her while doing the rounds to meet the team. Beth was in the hallway of the Denver courthouse, talking to Dan Abrams, one of my colleagues and NBC's legal affairs reporter. I introduced myself to Beth and received a clipped "Nice to meet you" in return.

At thirty-four, she was junior to her colleagues in age and trial experience, but I was impressed by how effortless she made it seem, how little nervousness she betrayed. She had an air of authority and confidence; she was easy with us, happy to mix it up and take on a reporter's ill-informed question or argument. Beth had many relationships in the news business, and she used them to spike inaccurate stories about the case on more than one occasion. During a tough cross-examination, she had a habit of placing her hands on her hips to betray incredulity, a gesture that was simultaneously feminine and effective.

Beth's memory of our meeting in the courtroom hallway is somewhat less complimentary. She remembers my gray pinstriped suit. "Big guy, big suit, loud" were her first impressions. "Big confidence. Young guy." It's true that I was young. She laughed when I told her my age—eight years younger than she was—but nevertheless, I did my best to impress her when I got the chance.

The second time we met was at a dinner, when a couple of the NBC reporters invited the prosecutors to an upscale steak frites place near the courthouse in downtown Denver. The restaurant was in a former bank, a huge, high-ceilinged room. We'd reserved a long side table. I asked the waiter to hand Beth a glass of champagne when she came in, and to say, "You must be with Mr. Gregory" as he seated her next to me. Her male colleagues rolled their eyes. Clearly, they thought I was the last person she would ever fall for. But she and I enjoyed ourselves that night, exchanging stories about events I'd covered and trial work she'd done.

I don't want to sound deeper than I was. She was attractive—petite, with stylishly cut brown hair and a voice that was low and sexy. I thought Beth had great legs when I watched her move around the courtroom during the team's interview of potential jurors, known as voir dire. She'd been a dancer in college, and it showed. She wore most of her skirts cut above the knee—appropriate enough for federal court, but as my high school English teacher decreed about the length of school essays: "Long enough to cover the essentials and short enough to be interesting."

There were qualities other than Beth's legs that drew me in. She was smart. That's kind of generic; lots of people are. But even from our quick chats during breaks in the hallway outside the courtroom, I could tell there was a toughness to her intelligence. She seemed to have the ability to see multiple sides to an issue, as trial lawyers should. And she wasn't easily intimidated. When McVeigh wrote her a mildly threatening note during the course of the trial, she barely reacted, in spite of how unusual it was for the defendant to single out a member of the prosecution team—not to mention the only woman on the team.

Yes, McVeigh was a mass murderer, but Beth had prosecuted violent criminals and Colombian drug lords as an assistant U.S. attorney for the Eastern District of New York. She knew not to let them get a rise out of her. She'd grown up in a military family and wasn't one to be shaken.

Watching her in the courtroom, I also saw Beth's

compassionate side. There was horrifying detail during the trial, especially as we heard about the nineteen infants and toddlers who were killed that day in the first-floor day-care center of the U.S. government complex in Oklahoma City. The image that dominated the front pages the day after the bombing was of fireman Chris Fields cradling the bloodied body of Baylee Almon, one year and one day old. She died hours later.

It was impossible to miss the prosecution team when they approached the courthouse each morning: The Denver police actually stopped traffic as they escorted the team from the office to the courtroom. Each day they would pass by the bullpen where the reporters and camera crews were jammed, sometimes as many as two hundred of us. The family members of bombing victims and survivors lined up outside the courthouse, too. Beth gave them hugs when she arrived. She had a close relationship with many of the family members and felt keenly the weight of their expectations.

The family members had all traveled from Oklahoma City for the trial, and they relied on one another a lot that spring. You could tell from watching them interact that they had become an extended family. For them, each day in the courthouse was tough. There were always grief counselors on hand. It was emotional for everyone. During the gripping testimonies from spouses and children of the federal agents killed by the bomb, the counselors handed out tissues to many, even some hardened reporters sitting in the journalist rows.

The trial still stands out for its courtroom drama. I'll

always remember the day when McVeigh's signature was matched with the signature on the rental agreement for the Ryder truck used in the bombing. The prosecution team literally pieced together letters, using McVeigh's handwriting from personal documents they had collected from his home to spell out the name Robert Kling, McVeigh's alias.

Another damning moment came when the owner of a Chinese restaurant took the stand. McVeigh had used his own name when he checked in to room 25 at the Dreamland Motel in Junction City, Kansas, but he'd ordered Chinese food from Hunan Palace in Junction City using the name Kling—the alias used to rent the Ryder truck. Yuhua Bai, the owner of Hunan Palace, testified that she took the phone order from "Kling" for moo goo gai pan and egg rolls that day. When McVeigh's lawyer said he was not familiar with the dish moo goo gai pan, Bai drew a laugh from the normally subdued courtroom when she responded: "Maybe you never eat Chinese food?" She pointed at McVeigh and said, "Ask him."

The emotional swings of the trial—the heartache and the evidence trail leading to McVeigh as the murderer—made covering the case a daily thrill. The emotional twist I hadn't planned for was one in which I was falling for the prosecutor.

I tried not to give away what I was feeling, but we reporters on the trial were spending a lot of time together, and at least a couple of them could tell I had a thing for Beth. They'd rib me about it, but no one took it seriously, because no one—including me—thought I had a chance with her. It was a conflict of interest for me, as a reporter on the story. If anything, that only heightened my infatuation. Whenever I got a page from Beth's office I always stopped what I was doing to return her call.

I was hoping it could be more than a call now and then, but we had to wait. Beth was more mature about that than I was. And she was obviously preoccupied. She had moved to Denver to work on the case, and she worked from eight in the morning until ten at night, seven days a week.

Beth felt enormous pressure to achieve the outcome they wanted. She was prosecuting an American citizen for killing his fellow citizens. If her team were successful, they would ask the jury to render the ultimate punishment: the death penalty. Not exactly the ideal environment for a romance. The survivors and family members were rightfully demanding; the judge in the case asked a lot of them; Washington was calling. Beth thought about almost nothing other than the case for the majority of that year.

I, however, had fallen in love.

Twenty-five months after the Oklahoma City bombing, Timothy McVeigh was convicted on all counts. President Bill Clinton called the verdict a "long-overdue day." I saw Beth from afar in the courtroom—she and the rest of the prosecution team were happy, but they knew they had to be focused on the penalty phase of the trial, still to come.

I was part of NBC's breaking-coverage team that afternoon, and I was working on a story about the conspiracy theories on the bombing. Many Americans—notably some victims' family members—believed that the government was hiding evidence. They thought there was another bomber behind the attack, or some foreign involvement. In twenty years, no evidence supporting those theories has come to light.

For the most part, McVeigh's guilty verdict brought nationwide emotional release. It was like a national panacea after the mockery of justice that was the O. J. Simpson trial. People poured out of neighboring office buildings and restaurants to cheer on and thank the prosecution team as they made the short walk from the courthouse back to their offices, escorted by police on horseback.

Beth figured prominently in the end of the McVeigh trial. The lead prosecutor had asked her to deliver part of the closing argument to the jury in the penalty phase, in which the government argued that he should receive the death penalty. Later, she admitted to me that she had memorized her statement and delivered it verbatim, which she doesn't generally like to do. But for this closely watched case, she wanted to be sure not to get a word wrong.

The courtroom was packed that day. Listening from the adjacent overflow room, I was struck by Beth's boldness. As a veteran herself—and the daughter of a career military man—she was unafraid to challenge McVeigh on his claims that he'd acted out of patriotism, as a former U.S. army soldier. Soldiers, even America's early patriots, picked a fair fight against other soldiers, Beth argued. They didn't target innocents, including children.

"Timothy McVeigh murdered more American citizens in one day than were killed in combat in the entire Persian Gulf War," she said in her closing argument. "So to call him . . . 'the most soldierly among us' is an insult to every man and woman who served in our armed services." That day, *The Washington Post* reported: "In a final burst of drama, prosecutor Beth Wilkinson closed the government's case by pointing at McVeigh and telling the jury: 'Look into the eyes of a coward and tell him you will have courage. Tell him you will speak with one unified voice as the moral conscience of the community and tell him he is no patriot. He is a traitor and he deserves to die.'"

Beth had weighed these words carefully. By calling the jury to act as the moral conscience of the community, she was saying that the American public expected the death penalty for McVeigh. She was also saying that by asking for it, the jury would be enacting the will of Oklahoma City and the nation; they wouldn't be acting alone. She thought it was important to show the jury that she could look into McVeigh's eyes and do what she was asking them to do.

As *The Washington Post* put it: "On an early summer afternoon in downtown Denver today, with hundreds of ordinary people waiting on Stout Street for the system McVeigh so despised to work its will, the jury agreed."

The death penalty had long been an important issue for Beth. She was raised to believe that it was morally wrong to execute criminals. Her mother, Judy, a deeply spiritual Methodist, is a pacifist. Beth remembers asking her mother whether she would kill someone in order to save her own daughter. Her mom's answer was no, somewhat surprising for a woman married to a career military man.

Judy's opinion matters a great deal to Beth. She modeled what Beth considers a truly spiritual life. She is a military wife who spent many months of the year alone—her husband, Beth's dad, is a career navy officer who would spend three to six months at a time at sea before he retired. He was stationed near a big submarine base in Connecticut, so most of Beth's childhood was spent amid the close-knit military community in the small town of Ledyard, Connecticut. With her husband at sea, Judy drew strength from her community and her faith.

Even though Beth didn't share her mother's commitment to pacifism, the issue of the death penalty was intertwined with her Christian sensibility. Months later, Beth told me she'd worried that her mom would be mortified to see her making the final appeal to put McVeigh to death. "Of course I told Mom about it, and I know she was proud of me," Beth said to me later. "But I'm not sure she told anyone at church, you know what I mean?"

When Beth was asked to join the prosecution team in the McVeigh case, it gave her pause, even though she was honored to be asked. She told herself, "You can't work on this if you can't get comfortable with the death penalty." Then she decided that if the government was ever going to execute anyone, the man responsible for 168 deaths should qualify.

•   •   •

The story of the Oklahoma City bombing didn't end there for Beth. Three months later, she was back in Denver for the trial of the second suspect in the bombing, Terry Nichols. Nichols, a drifter who shared Timothy McVeigh's anti-government views, met McVeigh during a short stint in the army. He helped assemble and construct the massive truck bomb that McVeigh detonated.

As much as I wanted to continue to cover the Oklahoma City bombing trials, the decision had been made for me when Beth reciprocated my interest. When my bureau chief at NBC told me that the network wanted me to return to Denver, I told one of the vice presidents for news that I was dating Beth. One of the assignment editors asked whether I could cover the trial from the viewpoint of the victims' families, but I insisted that NBC News shouldn't want me anywhere near a story in which my girlfriend was a principal player. I was still new to the network, and I didn't want any kind of controversial start. So it was decided: I left Denver to move back to Chicago, where I would be a general assignment reporter for NBC.

I welcomed any opportunity to make an impact on my NBC bosses up in New York. One way I found to do that was to sharpen my skills as a mimic and do impressions of NBC's best-known voices. I was proudest of my Tom Brokaw impersonation; I'll be honest and say it didn't come easily. It took real effort on my part to capture Tom's distinctive cadence and phrasing. Whether this was a good use of my time is up for debate.

Once I had it down, I readily performed my Tom for

my colleagues. Still, I was surprised to learn that Tom himself had heard about my impression. I was up in New York working on a story one afternoon when I got a call from the executive producer of *Nightly News,* directing me to attend that afternoon's meeting. A junior reporter based in the Midwest would have no reason to be invited to attend, so I rushed up to headquarters at 30 Rock.

The staff was sitting casually on the sofas and floor of the EP's office. I didn't know why I was there until the EP introduced me and said I had an impression to show them. I remember wondering nervously whether I shouldn't sound *too much* like Tom Brokaw in front of Tom Brokaw—that might annoy him, right? But my desire to get a laugh overwhelmed that concern, and I broke into my act, doing Tom in the anchor chair. Everyone in the room cracked up as I did some lines in his low and resonant voice—everyone other than Tom, that is. He was sitting very still, with a slight, knowing smile.

After I got back to Chicago, I was working in the bureau when a top-of-the-screen message pinged across my computer bearing the simple name Brokaw: "Just remember, your career is in my hands." He was joking, of course, but it was still a little terrifying.

I loved Chicago, though I was seldom there. Our Midwest bureau was small, just three correspondents who chased stories across a wide swath of the country. I spent most of my time traveling with a bureau producer in Kentucky and Iowa, reporting for *Today* and sometimes for

Nightly News. It made for a hectic life, because I also started traveling regularly to Denver to see Beth.

From her perspective, our relationship moved quickly from the stage when she didn't take it seriously at all, to a stage when she worried that if she did take it seriously, I might not. But I was serious. So serious that I told my mother early on, "This is it—she's the one. No doubt about it."

I found Beth's company invigorating. She was unafraid to challenge me if she'd had a different experience of something or if she disagreed with me. We often chuckled about our dissimilarities as we heard stories from each other's childhood. It's hard to get much further from my show business upbringing than Beth's rural childhood in a military town. I was attending opening-night parties after the theater in New York with my dad when I was ten years old. I loved amusing Beth with stories about visiting the comedian Red Buttons some Saturday afternoons; he'd welcome us in a velour jump suit and take us to his recreation room, its walls lined with photos. "There I am with the Champ!" he'd exclaim, pointing to a shot with Muhammad Ali.

I was impressed by Beth's academic rigor. After high school, she got a scholarship from the Army Reserve Officers' Training Corps, or ROTC, which funded her undergraduate education at Princeton. She was one of two women in her ROTC program at Princeton. When she once complained about the program to her father, he reminded her with little sympathy that military service was the family's only way to pay for her Ivy League education.

After graduating, she served four years at the Pentagon, working on special operations and intelligence in the office of the army's general counsel.

Beth grew up with a strong Protestant work ethic: She was taught to keep her head down and trust in what hard work would bring. "You have to pay your dues," she'd tell me. Her parents both valued public service—her father, the career navy officer; her mother, who devoted herself to local government and charitable work. Beth was raised to believe that was the highest form of vocation, and it is one reason she was proud to help bring justice for the Oklahoma City bombing.

The concept of public service was not as familiar to me, in spite of the fact that both my parents had worked hard to pull ahead. Beth quickly identified me as a planner, someone with a set path. I often talked to her about my goals at the network. As we spent more time together, I started to notice how rarely she did that. I knew she had lofty aspirations, too, but she didn't talk much about her ambition. She appeared more focused on the heft of the McVeigh experience than on what it could lead to for her. It's telling that Beth was inspired to enter the legal profession not by how well-to-do some corporate lawyers are but by a childhood affinity for *Perry Mason*. "People want to see you working hard," she'd tell me. "You should do work that makes your bosses look good rather than appearing to be out for yourself." I hadn't heard that advice often.

Sometime during 1997, I realized that Beth felt as seriously about me as I did about her, that we really might have a future together. I tried to visit her as often as I could, though this sometimes made for stressful days. I remember racing the clock one Friday to get from Chicago to Cincinnati to report a story, then back to Chicago and on a flight to Denver.

One weekend Beth came to see me in Chicago. I lived in a small apartment above a stylish women's clothing store in the historic Lincoln Park neighborhood. On Sunday morning, our breakfast was delicious strawberry-walnut bread at a little bakery near my apartment. Afterward, we decided to drive around the leafy northern suburbs of Winnetka and Wilmette to look at the fall foliage and houses we liked. When we got back to my place, we checked out the local listings and priced some out, to get a feel for what was in our range.

I worried aloud that day about when and how we would live in the same city. I wanted us to be in the same place after the Nichols trial was over. Beth assured me that she would move to Chicago to be with me. I was overjoyed; I think it was the first time I knew we were for real.

Not long after, we made dinner in my Chicago apartment one night, just a salad and pasta, and were sitting at my oval table in the bay window, overlooking a busy night on Armitage Avenue below. Over the last glasses of a bottle of wine, Beth teared up as she asked me whether I wanted to have children. I could see that this was fundamental to her. She was not going to stay with me if the answer was no. In spite of my young years, it wasn't even a question for me; I had always known I wanted to be a dad.

It was important to both of us that ours be a religious family. We were in a position to choose the tenor of our children's religious upbringing, and we wanted to get it right in a way that represented us both. As Beth and I talked, we realized that it sounded easier than it would probably be in practice. How would we choose our children's faith, and how would we define it for ourselves?

One thing I've realized in the decade or so I've spent thinking and talking about faith is that everyone has an instigating moment. For some, it's a tragedy or an inspiring event. Some of us have a specific person who does it for us—an instigator. For me, the instigator was Beth. Sometime before we moved to Washington, she issued the challenge that changed my life: "I know what you are, but what do you believe?"

When she first asked, I remember trying to locate the center of my faith so I could give her an answer. I found it elusive. I was Jewish and I believed in God; I didn't have much else to go on.

Her question coursed through conversations we had over weeks and months, about faith and what it says about who we are. It was a rolling dialogue that wove its way between us during car rides out of town; over coffee on Sunday mornings in Denver and Chicago; and during occasional Friday-night getaways at a favorite French bistro in New York. The conversations began casually and became more serious when we started to discuss marriage and children.

As I got to know Beth, I realized that she had a wider perspective about life and career than I did. Part of that was the age difference: I was only twenty-six, remember, which now seems too young for anything other than driving and cooking pasta. But some of what I saw in Beth stemmed from her deep faith. Her work ethic, her gracious treatment of people, her values, for example. When we began to learn about each other's religious upbringing, we saw that it might be the area of greatest dissimilarity between us—and that's saying a lot.

It took some time for me to grasp the full extent of Beth's spirituality, because she didn't speak with a recognizable faith vocabulary. Beth calls church "the centerpiece" of her childhood. Her mom, Judy, was an active member of the Gales Ferry United Methodist Church, and they almost never missed a Sunday service. Judy spent four of seven days a week engaged in church activities. Beth and her sister attended Sunday school each week. After services, Judy usually discussed the sermon with her daughters. They would spend the rest of their Sunday in an old-fashioned observance of the Sabbath: quiet time spent together as a family.

Church is not the full measure of Beth's spirituality. Her faith is located inside her. "It's just sort of all-encompassing," she says. "I feel that we are here for a higher purpose, and that guides us in how we live our lives every day."

For Judy, being a person of faith is lived through the small things. In her community, Judy is known for bringing extra cookies to coffee hours, paying regular visits to a convalescence home, and inviting for Thanksgiving dinner those who had nowhere else to go. Beth's instinct is to ask someone a question to put him or her at ease; to invite a neighbor for a meal; and to listen to a client's problem. She often makes room for a friend or a younger person at work, even at the expense of time she needs for herself. It's a practical kind of faith.

I'd always assumed that I would raise my kids Jewish. It felt like a core principle of who I am. It was strange to realize how vital this was to me, given that I wasn't especially observant. Coming as I did from parents of different religions, I didn't consider it a priority to marry a Jewish woman. But I did believe it was important to protect and maintain the four-thousand-year-old Jewish tradition as much as I could in my family. To raise my kids Christian would have felt like a betrayal of my father's expectations, and of my ideas about myself as a cultural Jew.

Beth could tell that I was not going to compromise readily, so she agreed to raise our children Jewish. Neither of us entertained the idea of her converting. But we agreed that it was important to choose a single tradition for the kids, even if it meant she'd hold a different faith. When they were older and left home, they could make their own decisions about what and how to practice, but we wanted to start them off with a straightforward spiritual identity.

Beth's concession came with a challenge, though. "If we're going to do this," she said, "we need to have a deep commitment to belief, not just culture. It has to be about more than being Jewish as a people." It's a challenge that has, in many ways, defined our family life. We agreed to mark out a path of spiritual commitment for our kids.

Beth was brought up with an ecumenical attitude to religion. Her parents urged Beth and her sister to attend services with their friends at the local Catholic church and Jewish synagogue, and to read from a series of books on major world religions that they had at home. Her parents' idea was that they should want to be Methodists rather than being forced into it. As a result, Beth tends to see the similarities between Judaism and Christianity rather than the differences.

Still, when we began to talk about adopting Judaism in our family, Beth struggled with some of the ways it differs from the Protestantism she grew up with. That fall in Denver, we made the mistake of going to High Holiday services at a Conservative Jewish synagogue. The rabbi's sermon was about the perils of interfaith marriage, based on the fear that some Jews feel about the wave of interfaith marriage in the Jewish community: Over 50 percent of Jews now marry outside their faith.

It was a terrible message for us to hear at the time, and an alienating experience for Beth. "I grew up going to church my entire life," she told me. "I never heard a sermon about who you should marry." The rabbi's words struck her as strange and unwelcoming, compared to the Christian desire to expand the flock that she was familiar with. She'd always considered the church's welcoming evangelism a spiritual act in and of itself. Even though we both knew that the rabbi's sermon was not representative of the Jewish experience, I had to acknowledge that Judaism can feel more exclusive. It is by and for peo-ple born Jews. It isn't as inherently open as most forms of Christianity. Beth and I struggled to imagine a way that she, my Christian wife, would fit into the Jewish family narrative we were planning to write.

The Terry Nichols case wrapped up in the winter of 1998. It wasn't as straightforward and dramatic as McVeigh's trial; the jury convicted Nichols of conspiracy and invol-untary manslaughter but found him not guilty of murder. Delivering closing arguments, Beth charged that Nichols made choices and was responsible for his actions. "He knew that death was a possibility and he didn't care," she said. The jury deadlocked over whether to sentence him to die; instead, a federal judge sentenced Terry Nichols to life in prison, without possibility of parole, for his role in the 1995 bombing.

That winter, Beth and I moved to Washington, D.C. It was a good place for both of us—I wanted to start covering politics, and I felt fortunate to get assigned to NBC's Washington bureau. It was during the coverage of the Monica Lewinsky scandal, so there was plenty of Washington intrigue to learn from and report on. Beth and I rented a small yellow house in one of the close-in suburbs of Maryland. We wanted to live together for a while before taking the step of marriage. Because Beth had been married before, and because my parents had divorced when I was young, neither of us wanted to rush into anything.

By the following year, we felt sure. We set the date for June 2000 in Nantucket, a place where Beth had many great childhood memories. She and her family visited the island every summer, and although their accommodations were never grand, hers was one of many New England families who enjoyed its beaches and lobster.

We had neither a Christian nor a Jewish wedding; we were married by a judge who was a friend and a mentor of Beth's. We wanted our service to mark out the life of strong belief we hoped to create together. We opened with the Lord's Prayer, which Beth recited every Sunday of her childhood, and then my friend Corey read a passage from the Talmud.

Near the conclusion of the service, we asked our friends and family to join us in singing the hymn "For the Beauty of the Earth," which gives thanks to God for creating the world:

For the beauty of the earth,
For the beauty of the skies,
For the love which from our birth
Over and around us lies . . .
Lord of all, to thee we raise
This our hymn of grateful praise.

Our wedding foreshadowed a life of religious compromise. Our faith life remains a work in progress, but it is also a blessing: the coming together of two very different worlds.

CHAPTER 3

Purpose

My Jewish Education

—————————✴—————————

As a family, we welcome Shabbat every Friday night that we can. We begin our celebration of the Jewish Sabbath around the dinner table, with this simple meditation that I read aloud from my prayer book:

> As I light these Shabbat candles, I feel the frenzied momentum of the week slowly draining from my body. I thank You, Creator, for the peace and relaxation of the Shabbat, for moments to redirect my energies toward those treasures in my life which I hold most dear.

We light three long white candlesticks, one for each of our children. The light flickers on the faces of my kids and my wife around the table, as the sun fades into the sky outside the dining room windows. These moments, before we pass the challah, or braided bread, that marks the beginning of the meal, feel like the exhalation of a long breath.

The meditation concludes: "Had You not in Your infinite wisdom created this Shabbat day, I may not have stopped in time."

Stopping time: That is an idea with great power for me. So often I feel like my life at home is like the UPS commercial—all logistics. Come Friday night, though, we are supposed to let all that go. Jewish law mandates that you limit activity, so Shabbat is a time to observe, not to build.

According to the Book of Genesis, God created "heaven and earth, the sea, and all that in them is" on the first six days, then rested on the seventh. It is one of God's Ten Commandments not to work on that day: "Remember the Sabbath day, to keep it holy. Six days you shall labor, and do all your work, but the seventh day is a Sabbath to the Lord your God." Christians observe the day of rest on Sunday; Jews mark it from sunset Friday to nightfall on Saturday. During this time, Orthodox Jews, who believe that Jewish law (or *halakhah*) is handed down directly from God, do not write, drive, or spend money.

Our family practices Reform Judaism, which modernizes Jewish traditions, so we observe Shabbat in our own way: just for several hours on Friday night. I actually like the idea of expanding it across an entire twenty-four-hour period, but my children are less enthusiastic. They would never put up with me imposing Jewish law on their Saturday, especially not my oldest, Max, because Saturdays and even Sundays are game days, and Max lives for baseball and basketball. But even in the several hours that we set aside, time seems to move differently. I love the sense of stopping to take stock of the week.

Life at a fast pace energizes me. That is what drew me to journalism, after all. But early in our marriage, Beth and I talked about how much we liked the idea of cultivating quiet. What we wanted to do was create a discrete period of time for shared family rest. It does not have to be a specifically religious time. It's just space to allow ourselves to breathe and think. To look at our children and notice how their faces are changing. To savor the food we eat.

When you make space for silence and contemplation, then you might hear what the Bible called "the still small voice." More often than not, God is in the whispers, as I was reminded by Cardinal Timothy Dolan, the archbishop of New York, when I met him at his office in midtown New York in summer 2014. He recounted the story about Elijah on the mountain from the Hebrew Scriptures. "Was it an earthquake? Was it fire? Was it lightning? Was it the storm? None of them," Cardinal Dolan said. "Then the Scripture says then a gentle breeze came by and Elijah fell to the ground."

In my Bible, this is how it reads: "After the earthquake—fire; but the Lord was not in the fire. And after the fire—a soft murmuring sound. When Elijah heard it, he wrapped his mantle about his face and went out and stood at the entrance of the cave. Then a voice addressed him: 'Why are you here, Elijah?'"

Making time to listen and hear—that's what we hope for our Shabbat dinners on Friday night. It is a structured time in which to slow down and pay more attention to one another than to our phones. It is time spent, as a friend put it after having the Shabbat meal with us, "talking about life, family, and easing into the spirit of the weekend."

Fitting religious practices into modern life is challenging for any family. When we first started trying to observe Shabbat, Max was five and the twins, Ava and Jed, were two. Which is to say even the most modest of goals was too ambitious for us. Could we get all three kids to stop screaming and sit on chairs pushed up to the counter just long enough to light the candles? Well, no, it turned out—at least initially, when they had no attention spans to speak of. Jed would get his hands on the challah bread and throw it across the room, and Max would chatter away as I tried to say the Hebrew prayers. My efforts to find even a moment of solemnity at the family "table" turned pretty consistently into a comedy of errors.

Unfortunately, I couldn't see the humor at first. I was eager and intense about the idea of marking the Sabbath. This had been my idea, and I felt a lot of pressure to get it right, especially since it was a new practice for me. We never did Shabbat dinners when I was growing up. For my dad, Judaism was something to be marked during the High Holidays and Passover. I'd been searching for a religious ritual for our family, and because this one didn't involve a long service, it seemed more realistic for a family with young kids—or so I thought.

I wish I could have been more lighthearted about the whole project. It's easier for me to let go a bit now that the kids are older and we have a few years of Shabbat dinners under our belt. In fact, we have even revived Jed's bread throwing and made it one of our Friday-night rituals. Beth will toss out a piece to each person at the table. It may not be the best manners, but it's worth it to keep the children engaged in what's going on at the table. When their friends join us for the meal, they think it's amusing to have their friend's mom throw food at them.

I think Beth finds it easier to feel at home in our Shabbat dinners than in other Jewish rituals, because she has her own strong emotional associations with the concept of marking the Sabbath. In her Methodist family, Sundays were always a day apart: the morning spent rejoicing at church and the afternoon resting at home.

Beth's Italian-American mother cooked everything from scratch six days a week; Sundays were her day off from the kitchen, especially if her husband was away at sea. As a result, Beth didn't grow up having the big formal Sunday dinners that many Christian families associate with the Sabbath. On the contrary, her mom took her daughters to McDonald's for lunch after church. These Sunday afternoons of fast food were a way for Beth's family to truly relax. Her mom's friends often joined them if their husbands were away on duty. The kids would have cheeseburgers and fries and run around while the moms talked. At home, Beth and her sister would read or play games.

It took a while for my efforts to stop time to move toward something meaningful. When Max began learning to say the blessing in Hebrew, it invoked an almost overwhelming rush of emotion in me. Watching my son lighting the Sabbath candles—his arm guided by Beth's hand when he was young—was deeply moving to me, and I was unable to explain why.

Recently, my friend Rachel Cowan, a Unitarian who converted to Judaism, helped me understand by saying, "It is a moment in which your souls connect." The idea made sense to me—that in those minutes, I am experiencing a deeper connection with my child. It's more than pride; it's about establishing a relationship between my family and God. As Rachel put it, "When he's hitting in Little League, you're proud and satisfied. But in that moment, you feel something that you usually don't allow through."

Come sundown on Friday nights, my kids shower and put on clothes just different enough to make it feel special. The religious texts call for us to "sanctify the Sabbath by choice meals, by beautiful garments," but I'm satisfied if they wear khakis and collared shirts. I often have a martini; I'm pretty sure that is recommended in the Talmud, though I haven't gotten around to verifying it. But I notice that if Beth and I have a drink together first, it feels different than if we have a drink together any other night. It's not that we talk about God or recite Scripture to one another; often our conversations are no more inspired than they normally would be. It's just that we have a "Shabbat consciousness," to adopt another of Rachel's phrases.

On the seventh day, God looked at the world around Him, surveyed His work, and said, "*Ki tov,* it is good." On Friday nights we echo Him by meeting as a family around a table to give thanks and talk about our week. I always take a moment to appreciate my blessings after we sit down. I look around the table at the children my wife and I created—each so different from the other, each quickly becoming a strong individual—I taste the challah and sip the red wine, and I remember: Yes, it is good.

In his wonderful 1951 book, *The Sabbath,* Rabbi Abraham Heschel describes Shabbat as an "ascent to the summit. It gives us the opportunity to sanctify time, to raise the good to the level of the holy." I consider our Friday-night dinners an act of love, a way to connect. These nights spent together will help protect us from the toughest experiences. For me, the ritual also represents my own ascent—the maturity of my spiritual life.

Why do I feel more Jewish than Christian, even though I feel more Christian than most Jews, with a Catholic mother and Protestant wife? Of course, I don't *really* know what it feels like to be Christian, but I do know that I sometimes feel a close kinship with Christianity in a way that many of my Jewish brethren do not. Experiencing Christianity through Beth, I've seen that the spiritual vocabulary of Christianity can be more personal and less abstract than a lot of Jewish prayer and religious identity.

What is it about our religious identity that sticks with us? Whether it is how often we attend church or how we self-identify on census forms, many of us make choices that are part of a complex equation making up our religious character. In fact, our religious character is increasingly the product of our own decision. About half of American adults have changed religious affiliation at least once during their lives. More than one in four American adults have changed their religious affiliation from that in which they were raised. Some make the switch because of interfaith marriage, but the bigger trend is that Americans, who once lived in tightly knit, ethnically, and religiously homogeneous communities, are moving away from them. For my own part, I haven't officially changed my religious affiliation—I just chose one of the two identities I was born with. The answer to why the Jewish identity stuck can probably be found in my dad's story.

Don Gregory grew up Don Ginsberg in the 1930s and '40s, on the Grand Concourse and 171st in the Bronx. That part of the Bronx was ethnically distinct or, as he puts it, "The only people not Jewish in my part of the Bronx were the building superintendents." (He adds, "They were Catholic," meaning Irish or Italian.) My dad still feels a certain amount of Bronx pride: "The Grand Concourse was the Fifth Avenue of the Bronx," he'll say. He watched from his window as Franklin D. Roosevelt campaigned in a car down the Grand Concourse in 1944.

Dad's father was born in the U.S., his mother in the Soviet Union. His mother's family were Russian immigrants from a village in Belarus that was leveled by the Nazis in 1941. My dad's father died of natural causes, when my dad was just four, which left a lasting impression on my dad's life. He felt awkward about not having a father and about being poor. After his dad died, his mom went to work for thirty-five dollars a week. Her brothers gave her groceries and paid her rent out of their earnings from the Shefrin Brothers delicatessen on Eighty-first and Columbus, which they ran, and which my dad remembers for the chopped steak sandwiches.

My dad's Jewishness was unquestioned and unquestionable; it was simply what everyone was in his part of the Bronx. My own Jewishness was not as obvious or simple, but growing up, I closely identified my own Jewish identity with my father's family in the Bronx. We called them "the New York family"—Aunt Dottie and her two kids. One of the two was Diane, who married Joe, a butcher. Every Passover, we'd visit Diane and Joe and their two kids in their high-rise apartment building in Riverdale, in the Bronx. I remember the building's heavy glass doors and the huge elevator call buttons. The building always smelled like someone cooking dinner.

Buddy Joe, as he was known to his friends, was a big man with thick hands and a heavy New York accent. He liked to show off his brute strength by pinching my wrist with his thumb and forefinger, a gesture that could force me to my knees; it hurt, in a playful way. Joe knew I loved New York, so he would lead me over to the big window in the living room, where you couldn't see the skyline, but the tip of the George Washington Bridge was just visible. Joe pointed out the Harlem River and the Hudson just beyond. Gazing out at the athletic field and the rows and rows of apartment buildings, I'd day-dream about the great expanse of the city and all the possibility of it.

Before we ate, Aunt Dottie, Diane's mother, would always pull Ci and me aside and hand us each a five-dollar bill. She said the same thing every single time: "Don't tell your father."

Being with them gave me a sense of what it was like for my dad to grow up feeling truly a part of a Jewish family. My dad's Jewish identity was never especially re-ligious, not even after his mother remarried an Ortho-dox Jew and his house became rule-bound. There was no TV during the Sabbath. His stepfather kept kosher, so at home Dad had to learn the complicated system of dietary laws known as *kashrut,* in which meat and dairy are never to be mixed, among other things. If anything, I think those Orthodox beliefs made Dad less religious, even if he never lost a sense of what it meant to be Jewish spiritually. He and his stepfather did not get along, and he resented having to abide by a new set of strict Jewish laws as a teenager.

"To me, Judaism is a feeling, not a religion," Dad said once. "I mean, I know it's a religion intellectually. But I'm saying it's a feeling you have."

My rabbi, Danny Zemel, who runs Temple Micah, the Reform synagogue that I attend in Washington, told me that this lack of religiosity is not uncommon among American Jews. "Most Jews see their Judaism as about observances and mandatory behaviors or forbidden behaviors," Rabbi Zemel tells me. "Jews, on the whole, have been trained to be spiritual skeptics."

Rabbi Zemel says that Jews come about that skepticism naturally. It is pervasive in American Jewish culture and can be symbolized by the thinking of one man, the theologian and rabbi Mordecai Kaplan. Kaplan may be best known for holding the first public celebration of a bat mitzvah in the United States, for his daughter Judith; until then, only Jewish boys had marked their coming of age publicly. Kaplan liked to see Judaism as an "eternally evolving" civilization, with religion as just one part of it. He basically taught that you can do Judaism without God. Kaplan's views were so controversial that they got him excommunicated by the Union of Orthodox Rabbis in 1945.

Nonetheless, he made his mark. One in five American Jews describe themselves as atheist, agnostic, or "nothing in particular," according to a 2013 Pew Research Center survey. My father is not among those who consider themselves atheist, but talking about God makes him a little uncomfortable. "If someone said do you believe in God, I would say, 'Yeah.' I wouldn't even hesitate," Dad says. "But to start saying why I believe in God and how I believe in God, that's not for me. It's just that He's there."

I don't think my dad prays much as an adult, but he once told me a lovely story about praying as a child. Dad didn't have his own bike, but his mom sometimes took him to a shop on 167th Street in the Bronx that rented bicycles by the hour. An hour on a bicycle on a Sunday morning was one of life's greatest pleasures for my father, age eight, followed by other typically Jewish Sunday pleasures—a movie and Chinese food.

"I never knew if the bike shop was going to be open on Sundays," Dad told me. "As we would approach, I had a ritual. I would say, Please, dear God, let him be open. I would cross my fingers and kiss them. And sometimes he was open and sometimes he wasn't . . . which is the way."

It could seem that Dad left much of his strictly Jewish identity behind him when he dropped out of the University of Connecticut and moved out west to become an actor. He abandoned the strict kosher ways of his stepfather's house. He stopped speaking to his stepfather and rarely wrote to his mother. He started going by Gregory instead of Ginsberg. In spite of all that, the Jewish feeling stayed with Dad. He continued to attend synagogue services on the High Holidays, and to fast on Yom Kippur, the Day of Atonement.

There's a Hebrew phrase my father used to say to Ci and me: *L'dor va'dor,* which means "from generation to generation." To me, this phrase marks out who we are together and what we share. I know my dad was pleased that Mom gave him "a clear field for Judaism," as he puts it, when it came to our religious education. Recently, he told me that he considers it something of an accomplishment that my sister and I have embraced Judaism in our own families. "The fact that your faith has become so important to you, I take it as evidence that I did something right," Dad said. "And now you're doing the same thing with your kids."

Really, Dad is the author of my story. I was born into a Jewish identity. It is part of me, and I am part of the Jewish story of a people who have survived against the odds for thousands of years. Dad never sat us down and told us, "Here's how a good Jew acts" or "These are the premises of our beliefs." We absorbed his Jewish identity more through osmosis. Dad's only religious requirements of Ci and me were that we should attend synagogue twice a year and Sunday school for four years, so that we could perform our bar and bat mitzvahs.

Although my bar mitzvah did not have the deeper religious meaning that my Judaism took on for me later, it was an important marker for me. I was aware that this was the moment in which I was joining the wider Jewish community. At the time, though, social stress was my dominant experience of the event. My presiding memories of the day are the white dinner jacket I proudly wore and the horror I felt when I discovered that one of the girls in my group of friends was having her bat mitzvah on the same day, which meant all the girls went to her party instead of mine.

I wouldn't say I thrived socially in high school. Los Angeles in the 1980s, as I experienced it, was not very different from the Southern California portrayed in the 1982 movie *Fast Times at Ridgemont High,* starring a young Sean Penn as a stoned, self-involved surfer with long blond hair. The L.A. culture that I knew was about status and conspicuous wealth. It was about fast cars and scoring a leather jacket like the one from Michael Jackson's *Thriller* video—neither of which I had. I was still driving my sister's 1977 Volkswagen Rabbit with a red-and-white-plaid interior and a backseat that flooded in the rain. That was a great little car, don't get me wrong—I drove it hard, and it lasted a long time. But it wasn't the kind of car that bought you social capital at my high school. And though I may have longed for a convertible, for the record, I always thought the *Thriller* jacket looked ridiculous.

I doubt many people engage meaningfully with religion as teenagers. I certainly didn't. While I knew many Jews, hardly any were religious or spiritual, as far as I could tell. I remember staying over at our neighbors' house one summer night watching movies with Steve Golob, who was my age. When we woke up, his parents were gone for the day. I made us some eggs for breakfast, which I ate on the plate used for meat, along with a glass of milk, disturbing the rules of their kosher house; the Golobs were Conservative Jews. But I neither knew that they were kosher nor knew the rules. When Steve told me they would have to throw the plate away because it had been defiled, I was embarrassed and a little put off. I couldn't imagine following a set of rules so closely. It was alienating to think that this was the purer version of the Jewish faith. It seemed otherworldly, far removed from anything I knew.

Rabbi Scott Sperling is a bright spot in my religious

coming of age. The rabbi at L.A.'s Synagogue for the Performing Arts for seven years, he was one of the few people I knew who had dedicated himself to a life of faith. A warm man with a walrus mustache, he spoke about religion and values in an easy way, never moralizing. He was fun, too—he would play baseball with me on the grass during Sunday school, which I attended from age nine to thirteen. He'd offer accessible stories from the Bible, and he would cheer me on when I tried to impersonate the Dodgers' Steve Garvey at the plate.

You could say that with only one Jewish parent, I am a Jew by choice; I could have picked either identity for myself. Not so for my dad, due partly to generational differences and partly to his more solidly formed cultural identity. Dad remembers being called a "kike" and a "sheeny" when he worked at a granary during his first summer in college and during army basic training. That discrimination contributed to his decision to change his name to Gregory, which is one of the veils over my Jewishness. The most notable veil is my looks. At six-five, with a fair and freckled Irish complexion, I've always felt somewhat undercover in the Jewish community. Not to traffic in ethnic stereotypes, but my height is not the norm for my people. In recent years, when I've spoken to Jewish organizations, I've begun my remarks by saying, "Yes, I am." Invariably, the audience starts to chuckle slowly, and spouses turn to each other and say, "Who knew?"

Not having a strong religious background freed me in a way. It gave me the chance to build my own faith identity.

While many people stick with the religious traditions of their upbringing, Beth and I have been liberated by our interfaith life to create something new for our family. Ideally, that means we get to create something that works for us. In reality, it hasn't been that simple, as growing numbers of interfaith couples will know from their own experience.

I first began probing my Jewishness long before my marriage. When I was twenty-four and living in Sacramento, where I was a general reporter for the local station KCRA, I took off work on Yom Kippur to attend services at a local synagogue. Sacramento was a new city for me—I'd never been to the synagogue and knew no one there. It was a pleasant space, with large windows that the sun was coming through. But as I listened to the service, I felt kind of empty. What does this mean to me? I thought. Why is this actually important to me?

When I called my dad to wish him a happy holiday that morning, I made the mistake of telling him that I didn't plan to fast. He was disappointed. "I can't tell you what to do, but I think it's really important that you keep that ritual up," he told me.

I knew that I wouldn't have been fasting for the right reason. What is the point? I remember I thought. Is it only for my dad?

I resolved to figure out what being Jewish meant to me.

My exploration of my faith and identity was not a straight path. It meandered. At first I thought that I might want to get involved in the Jewish community, maybe to delve into policy-related questions around Israel. I knew I wanted to engage more deeply with something in the realm of religion, but I didn't know what. I didn't think I was about to launch into a personal quest to bring God into my life—frankly, that would have seemed strange. I held many conversations but found no single answer until I sat down at a rickety table in a little patch of sun for a cup of coffee on a gorgeous September day in 2007.

A colleague had suggested I talk to a Jewish teacher in the area, a biblical scholar and Orthodox Jew named Erica Brown. We met outside a Starbucks not far from my house in D.C. and sat under an umbrella in the sun. Erica is small, with dark hair and a personable manner. She was dressed stylishly in professional clothes. Erica is "modern Orthodox," which means she engages with the secular world to some degree, but she observes Jewish law closely and isolates herself from mainstream America in some ways. Erica does not watch TV; she did not recognize me when we met, which I considered one of her many charms. Also, her Orthodox beliefs dictate that she should not touch men other than her husband or son, so I was not supposed to shake her hand.

"So how can I help you?" Erica asked. An innocuous question, but I found myself becoming emotional as I tried to describe my feelings about spirituality and family. I described to her my urge to know more about Judaism and the Bible, and I told her that I was trying to establish a religious life in an interfaith family.

To my surprise, I quickly felt at ease with Erica. She projects something that I can only describe as a sense of soulful wellness, a quality that stems from living a deeply felt religious life. I was not able to articulate my own spiritual desires, but I felt clear that Erica would help me define my journey.

Erica suggested that I might find what I was looking for by turning inward, to my heart, to God, and to the Bible. She had been teaching the Bible to different groups of people for twenty-five years, she told me, in both academic and religious settings, and she said she still found growth and meaning from it. I had a feeling that by reading the Hebrew Scriptures with her, I would learn something more than the meanings of the texts.

"There are thirty-nine books in the Hebrew Scriptures," Erica told me. "We better get started."

We began meeting every week in Starbucks or my office with our Bibles, and we plowed through the first five books this way—from Genesis through Deuteronomy and some selections from Prophets. Erica talked me through the meaning of different passages, and I cut my teeth on the Hebrew a little. Erica joked that she was giving me "the Cliff Notes of Judaism," but Bible study became a serious undertaking for me. I was determined to become a literate Jew, to understand the Jewish story that I was a part of. Having decided to master what I could of the Hebrew Scriptures, I went after it with the discipline of a tennis player determined to improve his game. Some of my friends were taken aback by my newfound fervor. As one NBC colleague put it: "I've never known anyone who made such a defined commitment for no apparent reason." His note of sardonic surprise was probably typical among people who knew me.

Erica sympathized with my goal-oriented attitude, even though she knew that getting things "right" was somewhat at odds with the idea of a spiritual quest. As we studied together, we'd talk a little about our histories and families. In time, she helped me see that my concentrated intensity about Jewish learning was about other things. It was also about my own family life. I wanted to get this right, so religion could help me change the trajectory of my childhood and create a fresh story for Beth and me.

After several years of making our way through the Bible in this way, Erica suggested we take a slightly different approach. She began acting as a curator and picked out texts that had some kind of life relevancy for me. Her hope was that by handpicking passages from the Bible, she would be able to help me see the importance of integrating spiritual belief into every aspect of my daily life.

Erica had quickly spotted a dissonance between my home and work lives and was determined to help me fix that. She could see that with my kids, Beth, and my friends, I was trying to live a more thoughtful, caring life. At work, I was caught up in anxieties and negativity, and I found it more challenging to act in a deeply caring way.

Erica pressed me to start acting as a person of faith and integrity at work. She said it was especially important because I was operating in an "anti-spiritual environment," as she described the world of TV news. "Stand up to the toxicity of your business, and stand up to it with kindness," she told me.

Some months later, when my colleague Chris Matthews pitched an unflattering comment in my direction in print, I had what Erica considered the perfect opportunity to live my faith. A 2008 *New York Times* magazine article profiling the host of the MSNBC show *Hardball with Chris Matthews* described a scene in which Chris was boarding a Washington-bound flight with Tim Russert and Andrea Mitchell. If the flight went down, someone said, it would devastate the network's talent pool. To which Chris quipped that I was outside the plane, arranging for just that. The piece noted that it was "a common view around NBC that Gregory is trying out as a possible replacement for Matthews."

The writer, Mark Leibovich, contacted me to ask if I wanted to respond, and I said only, "I hadn't heard that. I'm quite sure he was joking." But it stung. When Erica suggested that I write Chris and tell him that it wasn't a big deal, I recoiled from the idea. "Why should I do that? My heart wouldn't be in it," I said.

To which Erica recited a Hebrew saying: *Mitoch shelo lishma ba lishma*. "If you do something but not for its own sake, you will come to do it for the sake of it."

Sure, I thought, that makes sense. It probably is true that if you do the right thing even when you don't believe it, your heart will eventually become dedicated to doing things for the right reason. I totally agreed with her *in theory* that it was more important to be kind to those who were not kind to me. But that didn't mean I was ready to take the high road.

Eventually, I came around. Chris's comment about me was a small thing. The bigger point was that the piece was tough on Chris. I realized that it was a meaningful time to be supportive. So I wrote Chris a note, saying something like "That piece was unwarranted. Please know that I don't pay any attention to the story about me. I'm sure that's not how you meant it. I'm not going to give it another thought."

I ran into Chris later at the NBC bureau, and he made a point of thanking me. After that, things between us felt different. We became closer. And when I left NBC, he wrote me a warm and supportive note that lifted my spirits.

Soon after Erica started studying with me, she asked me a series of questions that I found hard to answer. "Who would you be if you lost it all? Would you be able to handle it? What kind of person would you be without it all?"

My best answer at the time was rather unsatisfying: "I don't know."

So much of my identity was wrapped up in my occupation. I was a journalist; I was on TV; I was going places. That's who I was. My faith was something separate. Erica wanted to make me think about these questions, not because there was any sign at the time that I might leave NBC but because she wanted me to contemplate my bigger identity. "You are not all the things that are around you, the trappings, the celebrity," she told me. "What you get to decide is who you are."

This growth was difficult, but it felt right, and I'm still on the path. As much as I was interested in the Jewish story and figuring out my place in it, I was also realizing that I had a spiritual longing—and that filling it would make me a better, kinder, fuller person.

Erica is a natural teacher, the unusual person who takes great joy in watching others grow. She has consistently refused to be paid for her time. Not only that, but when I have wanted to embrace Erica, to thank her for her kindness, I have not been able to. While we are both Jewish, the Orthodox rules keep me from hugging her in spite of our emotional closeness. Honestly, sometimes religion doesn't make sense to me.

When former *Meet the Press* moderator Tim Russert died suddenly in 2008, I found myself turning to texts from the Bible for guidance and comfort. We were all shocked in the newsroom that day. Tim was a life force. He'd been a mentor to me, both as a newsman who couldn't get enough of the political events of the day, and also as a man who loved being a dad.

Sometimes when I was covering George W. Bush's White House, Tim would call me at my desk at the White House and whisper down the line, "Hey, it's Tim. How they doin'?" Even though he was calling from his desk at NBC and there was no need to whisper, he liked to heighten the drama by lowering his voice. He loved it when I could give him some new tidbit about how the president was thinking.

I'd often pop in to see Tim in his corner office of the NBC newsroom. One thing for sure with Tim was that unless he was on the phone, you could always pop in. He would make time to talk about anything, but he would particularly light up if the topic was kids. I was impressed by Tim's dedication to fatherhood. It was striking, how much Tim missed Luke when his son went away to college. "It's important to be subtle about how much you love your kids as they get older," he told me. He admitted that he sometimes pretended he needed to be up in Boston, where Luke was at school. He'd call Luke and casually offer to take him and his buddies out to a steak dinner. He'd shell out for a big meal and watch the kids wolf down their steaks, just to be able to see his boy.

After I had Max in 2002, Tim called to cheer me on. "This will change you forever," he told me. "This is the best, and there's never anything better." When I'd see him around the building, he'd say, "How's the Max man?"

Once, when Max was about three years old, he and I were at a Nationals game, and we went over to visit "Uncle Tim." Tim had great baseball seats, right behind the Nats dugout. Tim was thrilled to see Max—he was there with a couple of his buddies, and he signaled to the catcher to throw up a ball. He caught it and handed it to Max, who took it, stared at it, and then threw it back down on the field. Tim and I looked at each other in shock. "What did he just do?" I said. Everyone cracked up, and Tim got the catcher to throw it back up. I wrote on the ball: "This is the ball that Max threw back."

In the weeks following Tim's death, rumors started circulating that I might be asked to step in to fill Russert's shoes, which was both flattering and humbling. It wasn't that I hadn't conceived of myself in the *Meet the Press* chair, because I had—it was a dream job for me—but it had always been just that, a dream. It was unimaginable to think that Tim would ever not be the host of the show. He was born to do it. When Tim died, it was hard to re-orient myself to the new world, in which Tim would not be on *Meet the Press,* but in which I might be the one to occupy the chair. My sadness at the loss of a mentor and a friend had another layer of emotional turbulence.

I soon realized that I would have to get used to being buffeted by public speculation and criticism. During this time, I asked Erica to recommend a text that could guide me through. She suggested that we read the Hebrew Bible story of Elijah and Elisha, in the Second Book of Kings, one of the great biblical stories of humility. It is about the great prophet Elijah, one of only two people whom God deems worthy enough to ascend to heaven without having to die. Elisha, his faithful disciple, knows it is his destiny to take on the prophesying work when Elijah goes to God. He will literally have to take up the prophet's mantle, the coat that Elijah used to part the waters. For Elisha, becoming a prophet is a daunting task, to put it mildly.

Before Elijah disappears up to heaven, he says to his disciple in 2 Kings 2:9, "Tell me what I may do for you, before I am taken from you." Elisha's answer held great significance for me at that particular time: "Please let me inherit a double share of your spirit."

In my world of TV news, I knew that I had a big undertaking ahead of me.

•   •   •

Danny Zemel, the rabbi of my synagogue, is a deeply spiritual man. He and I have talked a lot over the years about the growing secularism among American Jews; it is a trend that worries him.

Rabbi Zemel was raised in one of the oldest Conservative congregations in Chicago, the Anshe Emet synagogue, where his grandfather served as rabbi from 1929 to 1953. During that time, his grandfather took steps to include women in the prayer rituals. He was the first non-Reform rabbi to count women in the minyan, the quorum of ten adults needed for Jewish prayer. Traditionally, only men counted toward the quorum.

Rabbi Zemel attended Shabbat services every Friday of his childhood. He describes his upbringing as not only deeply religious but also inquiring and open-minded. One morning I met him for coffee at a place not far from his synagogue in Washington, to ask him a question I'd formulated for some of the faith leaders in my life: "How has faith saved you?" It's a heavy question, I admit, but I had a feeling the answer would be rich—especially from someone like Rabbi Zemel, one of the first on my list.

Rabbi Zemel began by saying, "Well, I guess first I feel very blessed that I've had very few moments of horrible crisis in my life." Then he turned, as many people might, to the death of his mother, which he said had happened twenty-one years ago that very week. She was diagnosed with a brain tumor and died only six weeks later. "So it was very fast," he said. "And my mother—we'd had a stormy relationship, but we were very close." After finding out the news, he began flying back and forth from

Chicago to see her every weekend, and he said he felt "very out of control, all over the place, couldn't focus."

Feeling worried, Rabbi Zemel called his mentor and teacher, Larry Hoffman, a rabbi in New York, who listened patiently. "And then he told me, 'Okay, Danny, this is what you do. Pick out a verse. And when things seem crazy, just say that prayer.' So I did that." The verse he picked out was from Psalm 121, "A song for ascents." "I turn my eyes to the mountains; from where will my help come? My help comes from the Lord, maker of heaven and earth."

Rabbi Zemel told me he recited those words to himself more times than he knew, and doing so helped him get through that trying time. It helped him remember "whatever the crisis is, whatever the storm of the moment, we've not yet lost our hope, because we cling to an eternal God."

My Jewish journey wouldn't naturally seem to lead to an evangelical Christian leader like Russell Moore. But my quest to deepen my spiritual practice goes beyond my faith. I have broad questions, and I want to ask them of many different faith leaders. Dr. Moore is president of the Southern Baptist Ethics and Religious Liberty Commission; although he is based in Nashville, he also has a brownstone on Capitol Hill where he works on policy issues.

Dr. Moore told me that his personal relationship with God began when he was twelve years old. He grew up attending Woolmarket Baptist Church in Biloxi, Mississippi, where his grandfather was a pastor. One Sunday night after services, walking the mile home alone and looking up at the stars, "I found that I couldn't distract myself from the words of the Gospel," as he phrased it. He told the Lord that he was lost and throwing himself on His mercy. That was the moment when Russell Moore says he was saved, by professing personal faith in Christ; soon after, he was baptized and received into his church. In his early twenties, he decided to heed what he felt was a calling to the ministry and began working as a youth pastor at Woolmarket.

I told him I was coming to him not for a journalistic interview but as a seeker, asking his counsel on how to draw closer to God. Dr. Moore said that in his years of ministering to congregations, he has heard many similar questions: "How do I strengthen my relationship with God?" or "Is God present all the time?" or "How do I see or feel Him more?" "These are the questions of our time," he said.

He told me that he typically hears either from people who have achieved great success or those who feel they have failed in some way. "People get to a point some-where in their thirties, forties, maybe early fifties, where they say either 'Everything that I have ever wanted has fallen apart. Now what?' Or 'Everything I've ever wanted has come true; now what? This can't be what I was put on the earth for.'"

Dr. Moore has what he calls an "orthodox Christian understanding" of the world, which means that he be-lieves we're all created from God, we're all sinners, and we're all offered redemption through Christ. Ultimately, he believes that a spiritual path alone is not enough—we must take the final step and accept Christ, if we are to find salvation. This is his answer when people come to him as seekers: Pray to hear God calling you to repent and to believe the Gospel. But, he said, while he believes everybody is born to receive Christ, he does not believe that it is something people can be argued into. "I don't think any of us come to Christ because we think our way there or because we earn our way there," he said. "I think the Spirit does something in our hearts that really frees us from a previous way of thinking."

My path as a Jew is not to accept Christ as my Lord and Savior. I do not plan to be "saved" in the evangelical Christian meaning of the term. But Dr. Moore's words had meaning for me. The idea of an emotional coming to God is something I've sought—and found, in my own way.

I would not say that everything I ever wanted in life came true when I set off on my search for deeper spirituality. But I was not outwardly lacking. I had worked hard, fallen in love, and built a life with a wonderful woman. Still, as our children began to grow, I'd surveyed the horizon and realized that something was lacking. It wasn't that I needed more from the world but, rather, that I expected more of myself. I began thinking of things I'd never thought of before: What does God expect of me? Where is God for me in my life?

One September morning, I had the fascinating experience of attending the Sunday service at Joel Osteen's mega-church in Houston, Texas. I'd watched his Sunday sermon on TV and was interested in his inspirational message and his everyman appeal to Christianity. So I was thrilled to get a chance to visit Lakewood Church, where more than forty-five thousand congregants attend services each week.

I was struck by the energy of the service. Pastor Joel and his wife, Victoria, move around the stage like rock stars in a concert hall. It's a rousing performance of music and dance, with a live soul and rock band, backed up by a gospel choir with dozens of members. It can only be described as a show. Toward the end of the service, eight female dancers took the stage along with a trapeze artist, of all things, who performed an aerial act, climbing a rope of chiffon up to the ceiling of the arena where the church makes its home. I couldn't stop myself from thinking: It's Cirque du Jesus!

Afterward, Pastor Joel spent close to an hour in the church lobby, greeting new congregants who lined up to meet him in the lobby after each service. He greets close to a thousand visitors each week; they come from other states and other parts of the world. On this Sunday, there was a delegation of Muslims from Africa. "People tend to think, He's the pastor of a big church, I can't meet him," Pastor Joel told me later. "I like to show them otherwise and be available to shake their hand. My dad started this church with just ninety members."

Much has changed since Pastor Joel's dad founded the church back in 1959. Joel Osteen Ministries has become an empire. His weekly sermon is broadcast into dozens of television markets and reaches a hundred million homes. Joel and Victoria Osteen take their show on the road multiple times a year. Over the last decade, they have held close to 150 "Night of Hope" worship events in cities around the world, filling arenas to capacity crowds.

You'd think anyone would be exhausted by a full morning of performing and greeting, but when Pastor Joel sat down with me over a cup of tea in his private suite, he sat straight at attention and looked me in the eye. He said lightheartedly that he'd developed a workout regimen and healthy eating habits in order to keep up his energy for the rigorous Sunday schedule.

Joel Osteen has a direct and affable manner. That, combined with his strong Texas drawl, gives the impression of a guy who is earnestly who he says he is: a simple man raised in the church.

I explained to him the desire I'd started feeling some years ago to go deeper into my religion. I said I had been enriched by exploring my Jewish roots, but I had struggled with the lack of overt spirituality in much of Judaism. "Jews don't like to talk about God as much as I like to talk about God," I said. I'd been on this journey to become a more spiritual person, I told him. It started with a desire to better understand my Jewishness, I said. Through Bible study, consultations with faith leaders, and a lot of trial and error, I'd created a strong faith practice for myself. Now I take great joy in regular prayer, such as a nighttime prayer that I say when I tuck in my youngest son, Jed, who is ten. It's sometimes called the "Bedtime Shema," and it is based on three biblical passages. I add some additional language based on other prayers and my own ideas. "May God bless you and protect you," I say. "May God lay you down in peace and raise you up to life renewed. May He help you find light when it's dark—and help you to grow and be happy." Then Jed will join me in saying, "Hear, O Israel, God is my God and God is one."

Sometimes I say that prayer to each of the kids, but Jed will not go to bed without hearing it. I'm sure as he gets older, his interest in a bedtime prayer with his daddy will fade. But for now, I love that he demands it of me each night. That prayer is a reminder of how fulfilling it has been to find a spiritual path that is nourishing to me and also suits my family.

As I told Pastor Joel that day, the hardest part for me may have been listening to what my soul or spirit needed. For many of us in the secular world, it can feel strange or uncomfortable to listen for our spiritual needs; we often do not know what we're trying to hear. For me, it continues to require real effort and personal understanding to be open to God.

Pastor Joel sighed sympathetically and leaned back slightly on the straight-backed floral sofa. He spoke his next words slowly, as though carefully thinking his response through even as he said it.

"I believe God created you with a void that every person has," he said. "When you ask yourself a question like 'How's your faith?,' I believe that getting closer to God happens when you call out to God in your quiet time. I believe God starts to reveal Himself to people like that."

• • •

One of the best lessons I've learned in my journey so far is that mastery is not realistic. That was a hard one for me. But there is no doubt that becoming the best at something is not the point. What's important is being open to receiving what God has to offer.

The lesson was driven home during a meeting with Cardinal Timothy Dolan at the Archdiocese of New York. Cardinal Dolan is one of the top Catholic bishops in the United States. I had interviewed him for *Meet the Press,* but this time there were no cameras. I'd come to ask him not about the Vatican's policy on gay marriage or the pope's proposed reforms but for answers to much more spiritual questions, questions that had long been important to me but that I had considered my private pursuit. Now I found myself able to talk freely about God to a man who had dedicated his life to the service of God. It was an exciting moment for me.

Cardinal Dolan greeted me in his red archbishop's cassock, a large pectoral cross dangling from his neck. We sat facing each other on formal leather sofas in front of a massive painting of the Vatican in an elaborate gold frame. In spite of the ceremony of his title—not to mention the orthodoxy of his beliefs, because he is known as one of the more conservative American bishops—he made me feel at home immediately. With his ruddy Irish face and warm, expansive manner, Cardinal Dolan has a way of making people laugh and drawing them close.

I told him that I had felt a yearning for greater meaning and purpose in my life for some years. "How do I open my heart fully and forge a relationship with God?" I asked him.

Even up on the twentieth floor of the archbishop's office, we could hear the hum of midtown Manhattan traffic. Inside, these sounds were met by the heavy organ of a Catholic Mass filtering through on a radio from a neighboring room.

Cardinal Dolan said something that I have thought of often in the time since we spoke. "One of the problems you may be facing is that you're looking at this as somewhat of a project, of a plan," he suggested. "And in the end, it's an act of faith and an act of love. A dare."

He said that he loves to quote Jesus telling his Apostles, in Luke 5:4, "Put out into the deep water and let your nets down for a catch," even though the fishermen had already been fishing all night and had caught nothing. But Jesus dared them to try again—to cast out to the deep. They took the dare and found that their nets filled up with fish.

In his book *The Sabbath,* Rabbi Heschel calls Shabbat a celebration of time. "Six days a week we live under the tyranny of things of space," he writes. "On the Sabbath we try to become attuned to holiness in time." As my family grew into the Friday-night dinner ritual, I began to see it not just as a slot of time in which to eat the food we needed to survive, but as valuable minutes and hours when we consider what it means to live with a sense of

Jewish purpose. I like to think there are many ways to achieve this: by being active, by seeking emotion, by seeking purpose, and by seeking goodness.

For some years, we've had a tradition of passing around a *tzedakah* box during our Shabbat meal. Giving *tzedakah,* which means donating work or money to charity, is a requirement in Judaism; there is a similar obligation to give "voluntary charity" in Islam, with a similar name, *sadaqah*. In our house, we hand out quarters to place in the box after we finish eating. Each of us takes a turn describing someone in our thoughts—a neighbor suffering from cancer, a classmate who has been sick, or an issue in the news that is upsetting one of us. We've had family discussions about everything from homelessness to war in Syria.

We do try to lighten it up sometimes. My kids have made me try out different ideas, experiment with ways to make the meal more enjoyable—and I'm glad for that, because, as Cardinal Dolan said, I need to make my religious life less of a project and more of a natural expression. Sometimes I ask Ava to lead us in a discussion. When Jed invited his friend Andrew over one night, we called his grandmother from the table and passed the phone around, because that's something Andrew does over Shabbat dinner at his house. But even if I am not waxing lyrical to the table about the spiritual meaning of our Shabbat dinners, I feel their meaning. I feel it just through the act of laying the dinner table carefully with tablecloth and napkins, and in setting out the challah and Manischewitz, the kosher wine that I sip on Friday nights for the sake of ritual.

Some time ago, Erica suggested that I read Psalm 119, which begins: "Happy are those whose way is blameless, who follow the teaching of the Lord." The psalm is a meditation on the law of God, and this line in particular stood out to me: "Your decrees are my delight, my intimate companions."

It's a strange construction. We don't usually think of laws as "intimate companions," as one translation of the Psalms puts it. But after the hard work to make Shabbat dinners fit into our family life, the idea rings true. By absorbing this biblical law into my life, I have learned how joyful it can be to celebrate God. And as Max says, it can be all the more joyful for everyone if I keep my religious readings and sentimental speeches short, and if I don't embarrass him by getting teary-eyed about it all.

CHAPTER 4

Transformation

The President's Important Question

————————✳————————

Whatever you think about President George W. Bush, one thing you can say about him is that his faith remained strong through even the darkest moments of his presidency, and he left office with his faith intact. As someone committed to strengthening my own belief, I have always been impressed by that fortitude.

Soon after I got the *Meet the Press* job in late 2008, I went to see President Bush. He was in the final weeks of his eight years in the White House; Barack Obama had just been swept into office on a wave of adulation, at a time of deep weariness about the war and of worry about the financial collapse. If President Bush felt he was being booted unceremoniously out of office, he didn't show it.

We met in the Oval Office, which he'd famously

decorated with a sunburst rug. There were two assistants with him, and when I arrived, he said to them, "Stand up straight, girls—here he is, *Meet the Press*." We sat down in front of the fireplace, me on one end of the couch, and he, leaning way back in his chair, as he likes to. After some pleasantries, he turned to me and declared: "Gregory, I want to tell you something. The economy's coming back. And when it comes back, it's coming back strong."

He held forth on the economy for a while, since we were in the throes of the financial collapse. Toward the end of the conversation, he asked me a question that he'd asked once or twice before: "How's your faith?" It might seem strange, to have the president of the United States ask such a personal question of someone reporting on his White House. It might even ring inappropriate, depending on your views of President Bush. But I didn't feel like he was trying to impose his views on me. Asking the question about my personal exploration was a way of connecting with me, just as he wanted to talk about my experience of fatherhood after my son was born.

The question also didn't come out of nowhere. President Bush had gone mountain biking with a guy in my men's Bible study group, the novelist Daniel Silva, who'd told the president that I was studying the Bible and getting serious about deepening my faith. So asking me "How's your faith?" was something Bush expected to devote a few moments to before moving on. It wasn't meant to be life-changing. Still, the directness and specificity of the question struck me each time he asked it. I'd never been asked such a straightforward question about my spiritual journey by anyone, neither before nor since.

Of course, I was aware of George Bush's reaffirmation of faith around the time of his fortieth birthday, which was also when he gave up drinking. I understood that he was a guy who had changed and matured a lot later in life, and he saw his religious belief as the centerpiece of that, as well as a source of personal transformation and discipline.

Seeing President Bush's faith acting as a source of personal transformation and discipline for him had been moving and encouraging to me. I was eager to share my experience with the president. I told him that I was trying to deepen my understanding of my Jewish faith, and to establish a direct line between it and my wife's Christian beliefs. Becoming closer to God made sense to me as both a parent and a husband, I said.

President Bush told me it was important to do that work, and he emphasized how meaningful it could be. He talked about needing his own faith more than ever at the end of his second term. "I'm in the Bible every day," he told me.

Ours was not a deep theological discussion. But it communicated several things to me: that finding God had made a huge difference in the actual events of Bush's own life; that he believed it to be a practice requiring discipline and effort; and that he found religion to be a regular source of strength and comfort.

Perhaps I was especially interested in Bush's experience because I had watched my mother battle her alcoholism. I knew my mom considered her twelve-step treatment program a spiritual guide for her life. The idea of faith as a guide for personal growth seemed positive and appealed to me because of my mom's experience.

By this point in Bush's presidency, there had long been debate over whether his faith had an outsize impact on his policies. Many Americans saw individual actions and policies, such as his pursuit of conservative jurists, his faith-based initiatives, and the wars in Afghanistan and Iraq, as all of a piece. They took them as evidence that President Bush was on an evangelical mission, or that he saw himself as an agent of God, taking orders from the Divine. Such concerns never seemed fair to me. I certainly didn't see the relationship between those ideas and his Christian belief.

Recently, I spoke to Jon Meacham, a biographer of the forty-first president, George H. W. Bush. He said this about the son of H.W.: "Those who were put off by George W. Bush's faith were probably put off by George W. Bush altogether. Like many politicians, Bush had the vices of his virtues. If you approved of what he was doing, it was seen as certitude and certainty and strength; if you disapproved, it was bullheaded, willful, and perhaps driven by a kind of religious fervor."

The argument that George W. Bush appealed to a Christian God, and was given an answer that in some way guided his policies as president, doesn't hold much water with me. He may have believed there was a divine plan for the world, but from what I could tell, his faith was more of a personal discipline. I think it offered him a source of comfort and strength in times of tough decisions, and it was not especially relevant to the outcome of those decisions, whatever you may think of them.

Before I left the Oval Office that day, the president made it clear that he would not agree to be my first interview on *Meet the Press*. That has always disappointed me; it was one of the reasons for my visit, after all. But President Bush did have some words of wisdom for me as I started the job: "Look, when you start this job, people are gonna knock you around. They're gonna say, 'He's no Russert.' And you just say, 'Yeah, that's fine. I'm just trying to be Gregory.'"

I thanked him. He was right about that. There are some things that are actually that simple.

I had a special relationship with our forty-third president. I covered his presidential campaign and all of the eight years he was in the White House, when I developed a reputation as one of his toughest interrogators. But I also had a jocular ease with him.

The time I covered President Bush was a formative time for me. I was developing as a reporter and maturing as a person. I was young, not even thirty, when I started covering George W. Bush's campaign in 2000. Coming to Washington with President Bush marked a significant moment in my career. I believe that the years when I covered President Bush rank as the most meaningful work I've ever done.

Even as I was having this foundational professional

experience, I was going through major life changes: Beth and I got married the year I started covering Bush. Two years later, we had Max, our oldest, and our twins were born in 2005. Becoming a father was indeed as Tim Russert had predicted—"the best and there's never anything better"—but it also forced me to confront childhood and personality struggles so they would not overly impact our family life.

When I was a young father, my biggest demon was my temper. I was slow to admit this; it was hard for me to acknowledge that I shared this unadmirable trait with my father. Having been afraid of my dad throughout much of my childhood, I didn't want to repeat that with my own children. But I couldn't wish it away. As Max started to crawl and walk and make messes—the things that toddlers do—I acknowledged that my temper was something I would have to deal with. Even as I was trying to teach my son self-control, I was struggling to rein in my own instinct to respond with an angry word or gesture, and failing to set a good example of self-control.

I struggled with my temper at work, too. When I first started covering the White House, I didn't have the detachment or maturity that helps political reporters survive in Washington. I found it more frustrating than my reporter colleagues when we could not get a straight answer to our questions about White House policies. I was not good at handling the spin that comes with the politician-reporter cat-and-mouse game. When they would fail to admit something that we all knew to be true, it felt insulting, and sometimes I took it personally.

Too often I got riled up about it, which was silly, since Washington press conferences specialize in *not* delivering straight answers.

When I got worked up in press conferences, it wasn't an act for the cameras; I wish I could have been that cool and calculating. No, I was genuinely hotheaded. I admit that more than once I slid a note of apology under Press Secretary Ari Fleischer's door when I felt I had gone after him too hard.

"Dogged questioner" became my persona as a White House reporter, though that had less to do with my reporting than with what happened during White House briefings. The cable news channels—especially FOX News—would replay my questions and debate whether I was too harsh on the president. Some took it as evidence that I was personally critical of his policies. But President Bush thought I was fair and told me so. Ari Fleischer once told *Politico,* "No one was a tougher, more aggressive questioner in the briefing room than David Gregory. But when it came time to go on the air, he was always nothing but fair." I wanted to separate out all the sausage making from what made it into my reports. That's what I thought the point was.

During the campaign summer of 2000 on a noisy tarmac in Ohio, I aggressively pushed Bush to answer questions about a *New York Times* article that had come out that day. It suggested that GOP insiders and party elders were fretting about the state of his presidential campaign. "Okay, cool it," he told me, but afterward, when we were standing around on the tarmac, he grabbed my arm with a smile and said, "I get it, Gregory. You're doing your job."

One especially memorable incident involving my persona as a reporter occurred during a White House press briefing in February 2006. Reeling with reports that Vice President Dick Cheney had accidentally shot a friend while out hunting, the White House did not make the incident public for nearly twenty-four hours. Nor did the White House release any details about the event, which happened while Cheney and his friend Harry Whittington were quail hunting on a ranch in South Texas.

We in the press corps found out about the incident not from the White House but from an article in a local Texas paper, the *Corpus Christi Caller-Times*. Like many of my colleagues, I was annoyed by the lack of transparency and felt the White House was not letting us do our jobs. I confronted Press Secretary Scott McClellan.

"Well, David, now you want to make this about you," he said, "and it's not about you, it's about what happened. And that's what I'm trying—"

"I'm sorry that you feel that way," I said.

Later, during the off-camera portion of the briefing, I said to him, "The vice president of the United States accidentally shoots a man, and he feels that it's appropriate for a ranch owner who would witness this to tell the local Corpus Christi newspaper and not the White House press corps at large?"

"David, hold on. The cameras aren't on right now," McClellan replied.

"Don't accuse me of trying to pose to the cameras,"

I told him. "Don't be a jerk to me personally when I'm asking you a serious question."

Okay, so I got a bit carried away.

After I calmed down, I decided I should write something for NBC's website, apologizing for my agitated behavior. That Sunday, Tim Russert asked me to come on *Meet the Press* to talk about the incident. I was happy to, because the White House was portraying it as a debate between the press corps and the administration, and I wanted to make it clear that the paucity of information about the incident was emblematic of the vice president's somewhat secretive style with the press and the public, and raised real questions. Toward the end of the show, Tim asked me about the back-and-forth I'd had with McClellan at the White House.

"I think it was inappropriate for me to lose my cool with the press secretary representing the president," I said. "I don't think it was professional of me. I was frustrated, but I think that you should never speak that way, as my wife reminded me."

I told Tim that I thought tension was healthy between the White House press corps and the administration—it seemed like the natural outcrop of a vibrant democracy. Later, I told *The Washington Post:* "This administration has put out press secretaries whose job is to stand there and not say anything. . . . I've been criticized by the left for being too cozy with Bush and not pushing hard enough in the run-up to the war, and criticized by the right for being disrespectful or hysterical or just going nuts over things that don't matter."

I still believe I was right to push the administration for more details that day. However, the incident helped me realize that I would have to modulate my temper if I was to thrive in the job, and in the business more generally. Looking back at the years when I covered the White House, I see that I was often too amped up. It's one thing to be probing and even aggressive. But there's no need to get angry about it. That doesn't make the journalism better.

The week after I apologized on *Meet the Press,* I received a note from President George W. Bush, handwritten in Sharpie pen—his favored means of communication—telling me he thought it was classy to apologize over the VP "flap," as he called it. He added: "It speaks to your character." That note describes something of my relationship with President Bush. Even if I had a forceful persona in the pressroom, he still reached out in personal ways.

President Bush was famous for his personable relationships with his staff and others. "I'm a people person," he used to say. When he decided he liked you, he'd find ways to make sure you knew it. When President Bush spoke to me, it was often with a half smile and some levity in his voice. It was as though he were saying, "I recognize what you are doing," even as he chided me or refused to answer my questions. Early on, he coined a nickname for me, "Stretch," because of my height. Maybe because he got to know me when I was so young, we had an ease between us.

Once, during the run-up to the war in Iraq, I trav-

eled with President Bush to Europe. During a press conference with Jacques Chirac, the president of France,
I asked Bush why he thought so many Europeans appeared to dislike him and his policies. Then I turned to
Chirac and asked him in French if he would like to comment, too.

It was as if I committed a war crime because I spoke
in French. President Bush took off his headset and said,
"Gregory, what are you doing? The guy memorizes four
words in French, and he plays like he's intercontinen-
tal." I had studied in Paris, and I've always been proud
of my French-language skills and didn't want the whole
world thinking I spoke only four words of French, so I
added, "Well, I can go on . . ." President Bush said, "I'm
impressed—*que bueno*. Now I'm literate in two languages."

Later that week, Maureen Dowd put it well when
she said: "There is something bizarre about watching an
Andover-Yale-and-Harvard-educated president . . . have
a hissy fit because a reporter asks a legitimate question about European angst and talks to a Frenchman
in French." That explanation didn't appease the many
Americans who thought I was obnoxious or unpatriotic
for speaking French in France. I got so much hate mail
that I had to change my NBC email address.

The incident became something of a theme between
President Bush and me. After we got back from the trip,
he pointed me out to the senator and majority leader,
Tom Daschle, and said loudly for my benefit, "That's
the guy who spoke French to me." When the Canadian
prime minister came to the U.S. and addressed a ques-

tion in French during a press conference, President Bush caught my eye and cracked up. At other times, he'd avoid looking at me, sitting among the other reporters, and I knew it was because he didn't want to laugh.

George Walker Bush was baptized in a nondenominational chapel in New Haven on the campus of Yale University and grew up attending mainline Protestant churches in the Texas cities of his youth, Midland and Houston. When he married Laura Welch, they joined her Methodist church in Midland and have stayed Methodists ever since. In Bush's 2010 memoir, he wrote, "Religion had always been a part of my life, but I wasn't really a believer. Religion was more of a tradition than a spiritual experience. I was listening but not hearing."

President Bush avoids using the phrase "born again" to describe his religious transformation. That implies a moment of epiphany, and he prefers to characterize his path as "a journey toward greater understanding," the phrase he used in *Decision Points*. It happened over time. The "seed" was planted during the summer of 1985, when the evangelical Christian leader Reverend Billy Graham visited the Bush family in Maine. "That weekend my faith took on new meaning," Bush wrote in his first memoir, *A Charge to Keep: My Journey to the White House*. "It was the beginning of a new walk where I would recommit my heart to Jesus Christ."

One of the things George W. Bush says he learned from Reverend Graham is that, while there is nothing wrong with using the Bible as a guide to self-improvement, that is "not the point of the Bible," as he wrote in *Decision Points*. "The center of Christianity is not the self. It is Christ." He began to think about the life of Jesus as a model for his own. He joined a men's Bible study club with some friends in Midland and started to apply the lessons of the Bible to his everyday life.

A year later, George W. Bush gave up drinking. He woke up with a hangover the morning after his fortieth birthday and announced to Laura that he was done. "I could not have quit drinking without faith," he wrote in *Decision Points*. "I also don't think my faith would be as strong if I hadn't quit drinking. I believe God helped open my eyes, which were closing because of booze."

Giving up drinking is just one piece of evidence that reaffirming his Christianity wrought a major change in George W. Bush's life. Even as he began to believe that self-improvement was not the end goal of Christianity— that Christ was the end goal— his new vow of faith was bringing about a personal transformation. As Jon Meacham says, "If you spent forty years of your life in a not particularly focused way, and then at forty you make a decision to change your life, and at fifty-four, you're the president of the United States, it's probably going to create a certain confidence in whatever life code got you from forty to fifty-four." If this life code is a formula that includes going to bed at nine-thirty, reading Scripture, and standing by a few clearly articulated principles, then we shouldn't be surprised that Bush stuck with it throughout his presidency, Meacham says.

In Laura Bush's 2010 memoir, *Spoken from the Heart*, she named several factors linked to her husband's decision to give up drinking: "It was the fact of turning forty; it was . . . the expectation that [the elder Mr. Bush] would run for president. . . . But it was also having talked with Billy Graham . . . and it was joining that Wednesday-night Bible study in Midland, which fixed George's mind on a higher purpose."

To me, that makes two things clear: George W. Bush's faith path was deeply personal, and it impacted every realm of his life.

I asked Michael Gerson, Bush's former speechwriter, to describe President Bush's faith. Gerson is an evangelical Christian with a degree in theology from the Christian liberal arts college Wheaton. He said that during his six years in the Bush White House, he came to see a man with a faith "that was not calculated. It was very close to the surface, nontheological, and had very much to do with his own personal journey."

Gerson told me an anecdote that seems emblematic of the impact of Bush's faith. It's a small thing, but it illustrates how he changed. "He could be tough with people," Gerson said. "That was his previous life. He confronted people easily." Early in his presidency, President Bush was preparing to give his first budget message to the U.S. Congress and was rehearsing with the teleprompter in the east wing of the family theater. The military communications guy in charge of the teleprompter messed it up, and the president lost his temper and left the theater, saying, "Call me when you get things in order."

It was only about a minute before President Bush came back in and apologized. "That's not the way the president of the United States should act," he said to the communications guy. To Mike Gerson, this was the act of a man who had undergone a profound transformation in his life. "His faith was a source of personal discipline for him," he told me. "And it was a source of connection with people." Michael Cromartie, of the think tank the Ethics and Public Policy Center, put it this way: "Bush's faith is a kind of evangelical, therapeutic religiosity. It's a personal story to tell."

George W. Bush struggled with how open to be about his religious beliefs throughout his political career. The *Dallas Morning News* reporter Wayne Slater, author of a best-selling biography of Bush, describes him as circumspect about his religious beliefs early in his career. As governor of Texas, Bush may have put forth policies that appealed to Christian conservatives, but he did not want to engage Slater or other reporters about his own faith journey. He told Slater in 1999: "I view my religion as personal. I want people to judge me on my deeds, not how I try to define myself as a religious person of words." In *A Charge to Keep,* published the same year, Bush wrote that faith could be misinterpreted in the political process: "I believe it is important to live my faith, not flaunt it."

By the time Bush launched his presidential bid, in June 1999, "he had gained confidence that he could talk publicly about God and faith in his life without sounding preachy or politically opportunistic," Slater wrote. In fact, when George W. Bush was asked to name his favorite philosopher during a 2000 Republican presidential debate, he famously responded: "Christ, because He changed my heart." Asked to expand, he said, "Well, if they don't know, it's going to be hard to explain. When you turn your heart and your life over to Christ, when you accept Christ as the savior, it changes your heart. It changes your life. And that's what happened to me."

Mike Gerson believes that this moment is telling of Bush's belief, in that it is uncalculated, almost unselfconscious. But in at least this way it was premeditated: George W. Bush had decided to be up front about his faith. It was part and parcel of who he was, and he was going to incorporate it into his political persona.

The evangelical community made no secret of how pleased they were to have someone speaking a clear Christian language in that debate, and they were unequivocally enthusiastic when George W. Bush won the Republican nomination. To many other Americans, this Christian vocabulary felt exclusive. They didn't understand or sympathize with it.

Other U.S. presidents have appealed to their faith and to God throughout the country's history. Invocations of the Almighty were part of the ambient atmosphere even through the era of Lyndon Johnson, in the late sixties. In his book *American Gospel: God, the Founding Fathers, and the Making of a Nation,* Jon Meacham says that God is "an essential character in the American drama" because He is "spoken on and called on and prayed to in the public sphere." Dwight Eisenhower frequently opened Cabinet meetings with prayers. Abraham Lincoln considered the Civil War an act of "divine will," one of God's mysteries. Much later, President Jimmy Carter proudly referred to himself as both an evangelical and a born-again Christian and spoke of Jesus' commitment to human rights.

None of these expressions of religion in the public sphere was as controversial as those expressed by our forty-third president. President Bush's detractors point to the religious references sprinkled liberally into his speeches and interviews as evidence of "over-the-top intrusion of religion into public policy," as Reverend Barry Lynn, director of Americans United for Separation of Church and State, put it in 2001. "Here is a man who seems to believe he was elected as the national pastor along with being elected to the presidency."

But Thomas Jefferson's famous "wall of separation between church and state" was designed, as Meacham points out, "to divide church from state, not religion from politics." In fact, Benjamin Franklin coined the concept of a "public religion," a concept embraced by the other Founding Fathers as distinguished from private expressions of religion at home. The Founding Fathers took care never to refer to this public God in overly Christian terms; they wanted God to unify the nation, not divide it. Even Jefferson—a figure claimed often by secularists—referred to the "Creator" and "Nature's God" in his draft of the Declaration of Independence.

More than at any other time, it is during war that America's leaders have called upon a greater power for solace and strength. If this country is built on the idea of an ecumenical public religion, we expect our presidents to act almost as pastors during moments of national trauma. George Washington liked to use the phrase "that Almighty Being who rules over the universe." His military orders were filled with references to the Almighty, including the less ecumenical term "Christian soldier." In 1865, two months before the end of the Civil War, Abraham Lincoln gave his second inaugural address, in which he made clear God's place in America's war: "Fondly do we hope—fervently do we pray—that this mighty scourge of war may speedily pass away. . . . Yet if God wills that it continue . . . so still it must be said: 'the judgments of the Lord, are true and righteous altogether.'"

On the night of D-day, in 1944, Franklin D. Roosevelt went on national radio as Allied troops landed in Normandy in an effort to liberate France. He asked the nation to pray with him, and read a speech that took the form of a prayer. "Almighty God," it began. "Our sons, pride of our Nation, this day have set upon a mighty endeavor, a struggle to preserve our Republic, our religion, and our civilization, and to set free a suffering humanity." He asked God to help America prevail "over the unholy forces of our enemy." And he ended with: "Thy will be done, Almighty God."

The attacks of September 11, 2001, began President George W. Bush's war. In the moments after those shocking attacks, he found himself forced to lead during an uncertain time. The first days afterward were some of the most harrowing of his presidency. He must have realized that this was the event on which his presidency would be judged. I was with the press corps on September 11 in Sarasota, Florida, where the president had traveled to promote his education agenda. President Bush was memorably reading to elementary schoolchildren when his chief of staff interrupted to whisper these words in his ear: "A second plane hit the second tower. America is under attack."

President Bush left immediately, and I and the rest of the press corps were stranded in Sarasota, watching with shock from afar as the events of that day unfolded in New York and Washington. The following day, we rode back to Washington in rented buses to join the team covering what was fast becoming the biggest story of our generation. A couple of days later, I flew to New York with the president.

Two days after the attacks, when reporters gathered in the Oval Office for a press briefing, everything was still deeply uncertain. How many were dead? Who was responsible for these four coordinated terrorist attacks? Were there more on the way?

President Bush seemed shaken. Toward the end of the briefing, *Christian Science Monitor* reporter Francine Kiefer asked him a personal question: "Could you give us a sense as to what kind of prayers you are thinking and where your heart is for yourself?" As he replied, President Bush's eyes welled with tears. "Well, I don't think of myself right now. I think about the families, the children."

He regained his composure and continued: "I am a loving guy, and I am also someone, however, who has got a job to do. And I intend to do it." He abruptly exited the room.

That question and his answer cut to the heart of who he was. This was President Bush's first public display of emotion since the attacks, and it reflected the sadness and shock that so many of us felt. The country felt deeply wounded. We had no way to predict the length and breadth of the war that was sure to come.

On September 14, which was declared a National Day of Prayer and Remembrance, I was part of a small group of reporters with President Bush as he toured Ground Zero. I was a few feet away when he walked out onto a pile of the smoldering rubble of the World Trade Center and grabbed a bullhorn. With a huge piece of twisted metal as his backdrop, he put his arm around retired FDNY firefighter Bob Beckwith.

President Bush shouted out a few words of an impromptu speech, and when someone in the crowd yelled that they couldn't hear him, he replied, "I can hear you!," with true passion in his voice. The crowd erupted in cheers, and he responded to their energy. He was truly lifted in that moment by the enthusiasm of the crowd. In the same electric tone, he continued, "The rest of the world hears you! And the people—and the people who knocked these buildings down will hear all of us soon."

The straight-talking Texas swagger for which some mocked him was, in that moment, completely honest. You could feel it: Here was a man in his element. He was doing what he believed was right and true, praising the men and women who had rushed to Ground Zero and put their own lives at risk.

This instinctive spontaneity captures some of the best of George W. Bush's presidency. After a few tentative initial reactions, once he found his way, he projected a sense of righteousness and moral outrage about the attacks. He called on us to "uphold the values of America." Whether or not he used words that referred directly to God, the meaning was the same. Within a matter of days, President Bush's approval rating soared to 90 percent.

Addressing Congress and the nation nine days after the attacks, the president spelled out the stakes. "The course of this conflict is not known, yet its outcome is certain. Freedom and fear, justice and cruelty, have always been at war, and we know that God is not neutral between them." His speech was interrupted thirty-one times by applause and cheering.

By calling on America's united beliefs and values, Bush blunted much of the criticism he might have faced. Still, there were concerns about the undefined war on terror and his "with us or against us" language. Even in this early stage, there was a healthy dose of skepticism about the foundations of President Bush's resolve.

Recently, I had a chance to ask Tony Blair about his experience of President Bush's faith. Blair, who served as Britain's prime minister until June 2007, worked with the president as closely as anyone during Bush's years in office. The United Kingdom was the U.S.'s closest ally, immediately signing on to the war on terror. On September 20, Prime Minister Blair flew to the U.S. and, standing beside President Bush in the Grand Foyer of the White House, he said: "My father's generation went through the experience of the Second World War, when Britain was under attack, during the days of the Blitz. And there was one nation and one people that, above all, stood side by side with us at that time. And that nation was America, and those people were the American people. And I say to you, we stand side by side with you now, without hesitation."

British forces were on the ground in Afghanistan alongside the U.S. military even before Operation Enduring Freedom began publicly on October 7, 2001. Two years later, the U.K. was among the nations that sent troops into Iraq alongside the U.S. to oust Saddam Hussein. Tony Blair joined the so-called coalition of the willing, the diminutive list of countries that made up the military command during the Iraq war.

Tony Blair and George W. Bush seemed to have many differences, including the fact that Blair came into politics through Britain's liberal Labour Party. But, thrown into world politics together at a time of great upheaval, they quickly discovered how much they shared. Like Bush, Blair considers his Christianity the cornerstone of his identity—he is a regular churchgoer and a reader of Scripture. Blair is up front about the fact that he came to religion and politics at the same time; he has said that what he first found appealing about the Labour Party was its core moral values. Blair took communion in the Anglican Church for the first time at the age of twenty, as a student at Oxford. In 2007 he converted to Catholicism, the religion of his wife and four children.

Another trait that Blair and Bush share is a sense of moral idealism, which each has linked to his religious conviction. This was visible in Blair's politics well before the attacks of 9/11 or the war in Iraq. In 1999 Tony Blair used the term "crusade" to urge intervention in Kosovo during the sectarian conflict there. In a 2009 biography of Blair's relationship with God, a former aide, John Burton, wrote that the prime minister was driven by the belief that good should triumph over evil: "It's very simple to explain the idea of Blair the Warrior. It was part of Tony living out his faith."

Burton's book is called *We Don't Do God,* and it gets its title from the words famously spoken by a key aide to Blair, Alastair Campbell, after an interviewer asked Blair a question about religion. Indeed, while Blair has not hidden his faith from public view, he, like Bush, was circumspect about it while in public office. Public displays of religiosity seem to be less acceptable in the U.K., where a 2014 poll found that just 8 percent of Britons describe themselves as very religious, with over 60 percent saying they were not religious at all. I asked Tony Blair about this when I met him in New York.

"I find talking about my faith very, very difficult," Blair told me, "because you are always aware of the fact that you're liable to misconstruction. But the truth is that if you are a person of faith, it's not something you leave at the door when you go out to work, because it's the defining part of your life."

The late-fall afternoon when Blair and I met was bitterly cold. We arrived at the same time in the midtown office where he'd asked me to meet him. He wore no overcoat, and said that he was better prepared for the weather in the Middle East, where he was headed the following evening.

Unlike President Bush, Tony Blair continues to be active in foreign policy. After he left office he served as the quartet representative for the Middle East, which made him the point person for an informal diplomatic contact group that consists of the United Nations, the U.S., the European Union, and Russia. He has established a faith foundation that tries to promote religious respect and understanding, and he also does significant private sector work through his strategic consulting firm.

Blair and I sat down in a formal boardroom with windows looking out on a patio where two sturdy potted plants were being buffeted in the wind. I asked him about the perception of President Bush as having conducted a "Christian crusade" against Muslims after September 11. It was clearly not the first time Blair had been asked the question. In fact, he's been answering it for over a decade.

"President Bush would occasionally use language which suggested his were not simply democratic values but basic values intrinsic to the nature of his faith," Blair told me. "However, I think you can take that too far. He was always very, very clear with me that we had to make sure that Muslims felt that this was a struggle for them."

Blair told me that, like Bush, he believed Saddam Hussein had weapons of mass destruction and needed to be stopped. But to many, there appeared to be more at work. In the lead-up to the 2003 invasion of Iraq, the idea took hold among some that President Bush had a messianic vision to attack Iraq. There was an oft-repeated anecdote about Bush and Blair praying together before deciding to invade, though it is not clear whether this actually happened.

Skeptics of the Iraq war pieced together different statements from President Bush to create a foreign policy that seemed to be centered on Christian belief: for example, Bush's line "I believe God wants me to be president," which he said to Richard Land, then president of the Southern Baptist Ethics and Religious Liberty Commission of the Southern Baptist Convention. But as Dr. Land explained on *Meet the Press* in 2005, that quote is incomplete. Bush went on to say, "But if that doesn't happen, that's okay. I am loved at home. And that's more important. I've seen the presidency up close and personal, and I know it's a sacrifice and not a reward, and I don't need it for personal validation."

Words that President Bush said to journalist Bob Woodward for his 2004 book, *Plan of Attack: The Definitive Account of the Decision to Invade Iraq,* had a similar impact: "Going into this period, I was praying for strength to do the Lord's will. I'm surely not going to justify the war based upon God. Understand that. Nevertheless, in my case, I pray to be as good a messenger of His will as possible."

When Woodward asked President Bush whether he consulted his father about the decision to go to war in Iraq in 2003—since George H. W. Bush had also made the decision to send U.S. troops into Iraq—Bush replied, "You know, he is the wrong father to appeal to in terms of strength. There is a higher father that I appeal to."

I think President Bush's faith gave him a certainty that made people uncomfortable. It made people wonder where and how much it affected the actions our president took. Ultimately, though, his religious belief was not an effort to make America a more Christian nation. It was about personal redemption and transformation. It was a code of personal discipline by which he lived. It infused everything he did.

It is this aspect of George W. Bush's faith that I am interested in knowing: the deeply felt religious belief that inspired a man to remake himself so completely, at the age of forty, that he became the president of the most powerful country in the world fifteen years later. Watching his faith in action influenced my own process of change.

Like President Bush, I came late to real belief. I was in my late thirties when I set off on the religious journey that has led to my personal transformation. Through my faith, I have learned about my failings, and how they impact the people around me, and why it matters to be better. I have tried to grow and change, even transform where necessary. I still fail, but I'm still committed to growing in faith and belief.

On that cold day in New York, I asked Tony Blair to explain how he balanced his strong faith with his decisions as a leader, since he'd said his belief was not something he could leave at the door. "In these large decisions, which really are matters of life and death for people in the security of your country and the world, that's where your faith can give you strength," he said.

"Not because you're necessarily right, by the way— you may be wrong, but somehow because of that alignment of the inner and the outer allowed you to take the decision on the basis of what you genuinely thought was right. And yet at the same time, it reminded you all the time that there is something greater, more important, than you."

I had the opportunity to talk to President Bush about his faith in January 2008, during his first trip to Israel as president, at the beginning of his final year in office. The trip was designed to breathe new life into the Israeli-Palestinian peace process. I focused on the peace talks during our interview, but toward the end, I asked the president a question closer to my heart: "Do you think people have misinterpreted what your faith means to you as a leader? And that maybe people think your faith makes you rigid in your thinking?"

"There may be some of that," President Bush replied. "I mean, there are people who aren't faith-filled people, who are suspicious of those who are. Because I guess they believe that I may think I'm better than them. Or, two, that somehow I don't make rational decisions. That they're decisions based upon some metaphysical presence. I tell people that my faith is a personal journey. That helps me find calm in the midst of the storm. That leads me to want to love a neighbor like I'd like to be loved myself."

George Bush had traveled to the Holy Land once before, in 1998. In *A Charge to Keep,* he wrote movingly about that trip, when he was accompanied by Laura and "four gentile governors—one Methodist, two Catholic, and a Mormon—and several Jewish-American friends." They all climbed up to the hill in northern Israel where Jesus is said to have delivered the Sermon on the Mount, the longest piece of teaching from the New Testament and the speech containing the central tenets of Christian discipleship.

Someone in the group suggested they read Scripture as they stood in that holy spot. President Bush chose instead to read his favorite hymn, "Amazing Grace." It stands out to me that this is what he wanted to hear as he stood on the Mount of Beatitudes. It is a hymn of redemption, of course, and it tells a simple story, a story that could be told of so many of us:

> *Amazing Grace, how sweet the sound, That saved*
> *a wretch like me. I once was lost but now am*
> *found, Was blind, but now I see.*

So often, it is just when we think we are getting better at something—really learning deep lessons about ourselves—that we find ourselves humbled. That's what happened to me in 2013, in an incident involving my temper that became so public, I didn't need to write the details down to remember them. Somebody else did that for me.

Like so many urban disputes that get blown out of

proportion, this one started over a parking space. When I got home from the NBC studios one afternoon, I found there was nowhere to park on my street. Visiting cars were clogging up the neighborhood and had been for days; there was a D.C. Design House event, in which a new home is decorated by local designers and showcased for the benefit of charity.

I parked farther down my street and started up the hill to confront the event organizers. I distinctly remember thinking that this was the wrong thing to do, then ignoring the thought. I'd had a bad day at work and had been carrying angst around all day. I told myself that my anger about the parking was justified.

Because it was a sunny spring day, the front door to the Design House was open and the organizers were gathered in the foyer. I found out later that I'd picked the media preview day to pitch a fit; the foyer was filled with local reporters as well as designers. They gave me some welcoming glances as I walked up, but these quickly turned to surprise when I made it clear I had come there not to admire the house but to complain. The event organizer approached me respectfully, and I told him loudly that residents hadn't been informed about the month-long event or how it would affect the neighborhood. His sympathetic expression disappeared, and he responded firmly that they had worked with the neighborhood commission to post signs, adding that you don't get to dictate who gets to park somewhere just because you live there.

I felt myself growing warmer at that rebuke and spoke back to him sharply. After an uncomfortable fifteen minutes of arguing, I stalked off. The damage was done, but I wasn't finished. I sought out my local neighborhood commissioner, who assured me that he was just as incensed as I was and promised to challenge them himself. Finally, I decided to let it go, but it was too late.

A couple of hours later, I got a call from my publicist, saying a reporter from *The Washington Post* wanted to speak to me about my argument at the D.C. Design House. I felt my heart beat faster. *Isn't this what they say in Washington?* I thought. *Don't ever do something you don't want to see written about on the front page of The Washington Post.* Well, now it was coming true for me. I'd channeled my inner Alec Baldwin and had a diva fit, and I was going to be called out publicly for it. When I spoke to the reporter, I tried to minimize the incident, but she minced no words: She informed me that she heard about such scenes only if they were really explosive.

I waited nervously for Beth to get home from the office that evening. I dreaded admitting what I had done, because this wasn't the first time I had let my temper get out of control. For years, Beth had reminded me to be aware that people were paying special attention to what I was doing and how I was treating people. "You cannot forget," she would always say, "that you are in the public eye. That requires you to be an even better version of your best self." This evening Beth tried to reassure me, telling me, "I love you, no matter what," but it was little solace at the time.

We had to go downtown to an MSNBC event that night, so I smiled through gritted teeth all night, worrying about what the paper would say the next morning. I found my friend Phil Griffin and told him what had happened, and his reaction made it clear that I'd messed up. "Tell me you're not the guy on TV who actually went over to complain about parking—at an event that benefits children's health," he said, laughing. "Seriously, could you be more ridiculous?"

"David Gregory Throws a Fit over Parking at D.C. Design House" was the headline in the *Post* article the next day. "Note to David Gregory," it began. "If cars are parked in front of your house for a month, send someone else to complain about it." Damn. Nothing worse than a critique that is accurate. Next time, maybe I'll stop and remind myself that if I'm going to act like an overblown Hollywood actor, I shouldn't do it at a charity event.

"If you realize that in the future you are likely to regret having been in rage, yet you do it anyway," the psychiatrist and rabbi Abraham Twerski has written, "you are announcing to all the world that you are a fool. Who would want to do that?"

Well, apparently, I did. Those words made me think twice when I read them some months after what has come to be known around my house as "the Design House incident." Over something so small, I suffered a blow to my credibility, and it was no one's fault but my own. The story spread on the Internet and local radio and set off many months of media criticism.

Nothing teaches a lesson quite like humiliation. True to form, my teacher, Erica, suggested that I apologize to the event organizer. True to form, I resisted doing so for months. I didn't want to write a self-flagellating note. I felt humiliated by the experience and simply wanted to put it away. But as Yom Kippur approached, I finally swallowed hard and wrote a note to the Realtor who had held the event, apologizing for my behavior that day. I told him that Yom Kippur is the time of year when Jews are supposed to atone for their sins, and I felt it was right to say I was sorry for my behavior. He very graciously accepted.

Perhaps the toughest lessons I've learned about anger have been at home. My clashes with Max have made a major impression on me over the years. I think of one incident in particular, when he was no more than six or seven, and I grabbed him angrily by the arm as I admonished him.

I immediately felt deeply disappointed in myself for grabbing him roughly. It was especially devastating because I was so concerned about repeating my father's intimidating behavior. After about half an hour, I collected myself and went back to Max's room. Max was sitting up in the top bunk of the bed he shared with Jed, surrounded by photos of hockey and baseball stars that he had ripped out of magazines and taped to the wall. I apologized to him, making it clear that dads can make mistakes and that I had failed to live up to the lessons I was trying to teach him and his brother and sister about self-control.

Max had some mature words of his own to offer me. It would be better if I gave him a consequence when I was mad at him, rather than pulling him, he said. "I don't like when you grab me like that," he told me calmly.

I was leaning against his dresser, speechless, as he said that. As brokenhearted as I felt at my behavior, there was something about Max's response that encouraged me. I never would have dared to tell my dad that I thought he was out of line. It was shocking—and pleasing—that Max felt he could say that to me. I know that he has discovered his father is flawed in many ways, but I hope he has also learned this lesson from me: that we should never stop trying to grow.

One way I have tried to grow is by turning to religious texts for inspiration. As a friend once said, sometimes our tradition knows more about us than we do. I find it inspiring that the sacred texts can teach us how to live as God expects us to live. Another thing that Abraham Twerski has said: "The sole purpose of Torah is the refinement of character."

Early on in our study together, Erica suggested we study a book called *Path of the Just,* a Hebrew guide to achieving virtue in your life; perhaps it is better described as an eighteenth-century self-help book. One part of the book is dedicated to understanding the different kinds of anger that people experience. The author, Rabbi Moshe Chaim Luzatto, makes it clear how destructive anger can be. The man who goes into a fury "would destroy the entire world if it were within his power to do so, for he is not in any way directed by reason and is as devoid of sensibility as any predatory beast."

It's hard for me not to think of the Incredible Hulk when I read that description. But it rings true, because anger can have the effect of overcoming all reason.

I know that as a parent, I would not grab my six-year-old's arm roughly unless I were overcome by a torrent of blinding emotion. Erica once suggested that I try to stop and pray when I felt a rush of anger coming on. Just pause, don't say a word, she suggested, hoping that if I did so, the anger would wash over me. I fail at this more than I succeed, I regret to say. It's hard to keep yourself from falling into a familiar pattern of behavior.

Still, it helps to notice it and stay aware. I started keeping a daily diary of temper-related incidents with my kids or Beth, or if I am short with a coworker. Recording it somewhere reminds me that I can do better. During the daily course of prayers, God asks us to repent three different times. I'm not committed to that particular ritual, but I like the idea of checking in with myself and reviewing my conduct. I like to think of Psalm 27: "Show me Your way, O Lord, and lead me on a level path because of my watchful foes."

Anger has always been my adversary, crouching just outside the door. We cannot make our adversaries disappear. All we can do is to refuse to let them in.

CHAPTER 5

Sacrifice

Will the Kids Be Jewish or Christian?

───────────────✳───────────────

When the rabbi of our synagogue decided to give a blessing to non-Jewish spouses on the holiest day of the Jewish calendar, it represented a major shift. You could call Rabbi Zemel an early adopter of interfaith practices; he started the tradition on Yom Kippur almost a decade ago, well before Beth and I joined his synagogue. Obviously, we weren't the first interfaith couple to walk through his door.

Only 39 percent of American Jews belong to a synagogue, according to the Pew Research Center, and the number attending regular Saturday services is significantly smaller—more like 10 percent. Outside of the Orthodox Jewish community, weekly synagogue has not been integrated successfully into American life. Most

Jews who attend do so only twice a year, on Yom Kippur and Rosh Hashanah.

"Saturday may be our worship day, but it is also Little League day in America" is how Rabbi Zemel describes the conundrum. He says it is such an institutional problem that there's a whole category of Jewish jokes dedicated to it: about rabbis inflating the number of worshippers who attend on Shabbat, and comparing how many of their congregants fall asleep during Shabbat services.

Because Temple Micah is not a large enough space to accommodate all the congregants, Rabbi Zemel decided to do the natural thing in multicultural America and mark the holiest of Jewish days in a Christian church. This had the strange effect of giving Beth an opportunity to visit a Methodist church twice a year for Jewish services. I can't say she is thrilled about this irony, but it seems somehow appropriate for our family, and it says something interesting about modern-day religious life in America.

The Metropolitan Memorial United Methodist Church is a somber, formal Gothic revival church. The sanctuary is dark in spite of the soaring ceiling—the gray stone seems to soak up what little light the long stained glass windows let in. On the Jewish High Holidays, the rabbis cover the crucifixes in the side chapels with linen and replace the gold cross above the altar with a Torah.

Yom Kippur services are long, beginning the night before the holiday and then running through most of the following day. Toward the end of the morning service, Rabbi Zemel invites the non-Jewish members of the congregation to come up into the chancel and stand at the monumental stone altar. During the Yom Kippur service, there were more than thirty non-Jewish spouses up there, including Beth. Then Rabbi Zemel reads these words: "You are an embodiment of the grace and beauty of this country where a Jew is actually someone that a person wants to marry and not some 'other' to be shunned. Many of you have made the historic and unprecedented decision to raise Jewish children. We will vow never to take this for granted. You come to services, even when it feels strange and confusing at first. You hum along to the Hebrew prayers, and some of you learn to read our ancient language. We know that some of you have paid a personal price for the generous decision you made to raise Jewish children, and giving up the joy of sharing your own spiritual beliefs and passing your own religious traditions down to your kids. Your presence here honors us. Your presence here makes us stronger and wiser."

He asks the congregation to rise so he can say a short ancient blessing from the Torah, and the Hebrew echoes through the cathedral. In spite of the formality of the church and the number of people in the pews—there are usually several hundred attendees at Yom Kippur services—the congregation always gets emotional at this moment. Beth cries every time she receives the blessing.

"This year I was thinking that the rabbis really understand the sacrifice we spouses have made," she told me after this year's service. "They know just how hard it is, because they are people of great faith themselves. Perhaps it would be even more difficult for them to make the same sacrifice and leave their religion because of what's happened to Jews over the centuries. But it means a great deal to me that they seem to know how I feel about the religion I grew up in."

It took Beth many years to acknowledge how much of a sacrifice it has been for her to give up raising our kids Christian. Having agreed early on to raise them Jewish, she never wanted to go back on her promise, because she thought that would be unfair and hurtful. As a result, the decision is not something she likes to examine over and over. It's a choice she made.

Beth believes Judaism brings many great values and rituals into our life, and she knows how important it was to me to pass it on to my own children. My Judaism was a cornerstone of my identity, and she was willing to accept it as our family identity, in spite of the obvious drawback for her—that she does not get to share her religious beliefs and traditions with her kids.

I'm happy to have a Christmas tree each year; I grew up having one. But Beth hasn't taken the kids to church on Christmas or Easter, because we thought it might confuse them to be exposed to both religions, at least when they were young. More recently, we've talked about changing that, which would be something of a compromise for me. In my own religious search, I've tried to focus more on the spiritual element than on the strictly ethnic part of my Jewish identity, since I knew it would be easier for her to come along with me.

But that doesn't mean it is all settled. Not by any stretch. In the writing and reporting of this book, we've both been forced to examine our faith lives more deeply, and to acknowledge that ours is a complicated picture. In the days following the Yom Kippur service, I asked Beth what it felt like this year to receive the blessing from Rabbi Zemel. We were outside on our patio, enjoying a strong late-October sun. I was in a wicker deck chair in my shirtsleeves, finishing a salad. Beth had been working from home that morning but was getting ready to leave for a meeting, so she had her handbag beside her, and she pulled out her sunglasses against the bright sun.

"You know, when I was up there at the altar this year," she said, "I was thinking, Why did I really do this? Because it's by far the biggest sacrifice I've ever made in my life." Beth had to stop here to wipe away her tears, but she quickly composed herself. She was determined to make her point. "And you know, it does not get easier. Like when Max is struggling with his Hebrew lessons—I can be supportive, but I can't actually help him. If I ask him to read the Hebrew to me, he'll say, 'But you don't even know what it means.' And he's right."

There have been signs along the way that deciding to be a Jewish family was difficult for Beth. Some years ago, I was standing with her at the counter of a department store on the Sunday before Christmas. She noticed a couple walking through the store with their children, all four of them dressed nicely, the little girl in a hat and dress shoes. They had clearly come from church. Beth turned to me and said, "The kids dress like that because they know that it is expected of them on Sundays. They comply because church is a regular part of their lives."

Her observation irritated me, and when we got back in the car, I told her so. It felt like a judgment on our life as a Jewish family, since we do not go to weekly synagogue services, and since we sometimes bemoan the fact that our kids complain whenever they have to wear something other than sweatpants. That's not how she meant it, though. Once I got over my annoyance and we were able to talk it through, I realized that what Beth was expressing was a generalized longing for the customs she associates with her own family and upbringing, particularly during the Christmas season.

As she stared ahead at the road, Beth told me for perhaps the first time that she had not understood how hard it would be to give up her faith for me. I was startled and somewhat alarmed to hear her say this. Of course, deep down I probably knew that it was difficult for her, but she didn't let on, and I didn't want to acknowledge it to myself. Thinking about what she had sacrificed made me feel guilty and responsible—not easy emotions to feel—so for the most part during our marriage, neither of us brought up her Christian faith. That has changed in recent years, as my faith journey has become a bigger part of my life.

Sitting on the patio that October day, Beth acknowledged something she hadn't told me before. "You know, I really did it for you, not for our children," she said. "I thought you needed a spiritual life. My own faith gives me strength and focus, and I wanted the person I love the most to have that, too."

Beth pushed her sunglasses up onto her head so she could dab her eyes. I was squinting hard against the sun, trying to read her face, and I saw a mixture of conflicting emotions there. Watching her, I felt loved and gratified but also burdened by the weight of what she has sacrificed.

Beth chuckled as she said she was aware that many Christians might not agree she is doing "the Christian thing" by giving up raising her children Christian: a great irony. But that is not the part that really bothers her.

"I think I was naive about this decision," she admitted. "I thought, This will be okay because I have my own faith. I'm not going to convert. This won't change who I am. But over time, I've come to feel it more, not sharing my religion with our kids. I don't get to show them how the church looks in the different seasons. I love how it is hung with different ornaments, the hymns we sing for each holiday—I used to be able to sing probably a hundred hymns just by memory. So . . . yes, it has come to feel like a loss."

I think that being a Jewish family is harder for Beth now that the kids are old enough to understand what it means and to see the difference between her and me. The first time Ava said to her, "But Mom, you're not even Jewish!," there was no mistaking how hurtful it was for Beth. I could tell from her expression that she was shocked and saddened to hear it so starkly. She has told me that she sometimes feels a pang of sadness to hear me describe the emotions I feel when I watch our kids lighting Shabbat candles and realize that this is our shared story. She loves that I share my religion with them, but it bothers her that she does not.

Though I should have seen it earlier, I allowed myself to look past her sadness because Beth didn't want to make a big deal about it. When I sensed it, I reminded myself that Beth still had her faith and could go to church whenever she wanted to. Now I understand that this approach oversimplified her sacrifice. We don't need to talk about it every week or even every month, but it's only fair to acknowledge it for what it is.

Some might say, "Well, if she really wanted to share the experience with our children, Beth could learn Hebrew; she could convert." But that's not fair. What I've been discovering on this journey is how intensely personal faith is.

Just as I feel an almost primal connection to my Jewish identity, so Beth feels linked to the Methodist church she grew up in. She doesn't attend church often anymore, because she wants to spend her weekends with me and the kids. But she talks about what she loves: the sound of the church bells before the service, which evokes her childhood. The hush of the room once everyone has settled into the pews, which marks it as a time for quiet and reflection. The music of the hymns, which inspires her. Perhaps most important is the welcoming demeanor of the ushers and pastors, which reminds Beth that this is her community. She once compared church on Sunday to a child clutching a security blanket: It gives an almost indescribable sensation of home.

For many of us, community is inseparable from re-

ligion. At Temple Micah, because there are many interfaith couples and it is such a spiritual place, I have
increasingly felt the warmth of connecting with a Jewish
community.

One Saturday morning in 2011, my friend Jeff and
I decided to go to services at Temple Micah, apropos of
nothing. Jeff is in my Bible study group, a loose collection
of ten or twelve of us, all Jewish men, mostly journalists.
We meet every few months, and I do not think any of us
attends weekly synagogue services. To our surprise, we
caught sight of our friend Steve, another journalist who
studies with us, lingering in the lobby area before the
services. He told us that his mother had died the night
before. He was alone because his wife and kids were out
of town, and he knew his mother would have wanted him
to go to synagogue that day. He looked shell-shocked, in
deep grief and need.

The three of us sat together during the service, and
I put my hand on Steve's shoulder during some of the
prayers, when it looked like he was struggling not to
weep. Later, Steve told me that it felt like "a gift from
somewhere" to run into us there. Jeff's phrase was "divine intervention."

To be there for someone who has just experienced
a loss and feels a longing to connect was a real moment
of grace for me. Jeff and I are not the kind of friends
Steve would have called after the death of his mother,
but he did not need to. We found him—and not in a
coffee shop but in a synagogue, where we sat and prayed
together.

The experience reminded me of the lesson in the Bible when God calls out to Abraham and Abraham says, "*Hineni*," which is translated as "Behold, here I am." But it conveys a deeper meaning: I am here with all my being, physically and spiritually. I am truly present. You can count on me.

It can be so awkward to talk to someone who has experienced the death of a loved one. But on this day, the most important thing we could communicate was that we were there for Steve.

The Southern Baptist leader Russell Moore once told me that his "church family" is so important to him that he keeps a framed shard of glass on his desk from a window that shattered in his childhood church in Biloxi, Mississippi. "The Bible makes it very clear that we're not isolated," he told me. "We're part of a household of brothers and sisters, and we're all weak in some points and strong in some points, and we 'bear each other up,' to use the language that the Bible uses."

He referred to Paul's letter in I Corinthians 12, in which Paul uses a metaphor of the parts of the body to describe the relationship between members of a congregation and the church as a whole: "There are many members, yet one body. The eye cannot say to the hand, 'I have no need of you,' nor again the hand to the feet, 'I have no need of you.' . . . If one member suffers, all suffer together with it; if one member is honored, all rejoice together with it."

•   •   •

My family and I continue to struggle to find a religious community that works for us. It took us many years to choose a Jewish institution. The first synagogue we joined back in 1998 seemed to tick all the right boxes: A sign outside welcomes new members. It is Reform. It holds "Tot Shabbats," Friday-night services and meals for young kids. It is open to non-Jewish spouses.

But Beth didn't feel welcome there. She couldn't forget an experience she had one day when she stopped into the synagogue with Max to drop off food supplies for a hunger drive. Some staff members and congregants were filling bags with supplies in one of the rooms, and they barely acknowledged her when she came in. When they did, they just grunted and gestured at a corner for her to drop the stuff.

"I didn't want a big hurrah," Beth told me later. "It wasn't about thanking us for the canned food we brought. But how about a hello? I mean, that's our community. Are we crazy to expect them to talk to us?"

I had to agree. It felt cold and unwelcoming. We set about looking for a new place to pray. In a way, Beth and I were "shul shopping." The shopping metaphor was apt, because I needed to see what was out there. We wanted a synagogue that was progressive enough to accept non-Jewish spouses who did not intend to convert. I was also hoping to find a spiritual Jewish leadership whom I could engage with. I wanted a synagogue where High Holiday services felt thoughtful and religious, about more than just the cultural identity.

We were also looking for a place where the kids

could learn about their Jewishness. Beth and I had decided to send them to Hebrew school, to help them prepare for their bar and bat mitzvah ceremonies. It follows the model of Christian Sunday school, which means it does not conflict with kids' Saturday activities. However, there is no sense of partnership with the parents in terms of the lived religious life. Christian Sunday school works because when the parents go to the sanctuary for the sermon, the children go to the classroom for an age-appropriate version of the same lesson. But when Jewish kids don't see their parents attending regular services, they can feel as though they are getting dropped off for a weekly inoculation.

One of the things I liked about Rabbi Danny Zemel was that he was forthright about this and other problems with modern-day American Reform Judaism. He didn't try to paper over the difficult issues, and he wasn't put off by my direct questions when I met him over coffee to talk about joining Temple Micah. He also made it clear that he didn't have the answers to all my questions. He calls Temple Micah "a smart, messy place with a soul," because, as he puts it, everything that is hard is messy.

"We're the heirs to an incredibly open-minded, liberal tradition," he says. "Judaism demands us to be idol smashers. And any given practice easily becomes an idol." Rabbi Zemel urges the Jewish community to come up with a new language of spirituality and meaning and a new theology that takes contemporary America into account.

Not long ago, we had a chance to see our rabbi

smashing idols. At a parent meeting for Max's bar mitzvah class, Rabbi Zemel mentioned that the non-Jewish parents of the child couldn't recite the blessing; only the child's Jewish relatives could stand up on the bimah. I raised my hand and said, "Okay, rabbi, so are you going to tell Beth she can't speak at her son's bar mitzvah, or am I?" Everyone laughed, but it upset me to imagine that Max, who identifies as Jewish, would have very few of his relatives beside him at his coming-of-age ceremony.

Some months later, Rabbi Zemel wrote me to say that after giving it some thought, he had decided to write a new blessing that non-Jewish relatives could read at bar and bat mitzvahs. He had labored over the language—both the Hebrew and the English—so that it would read as beautifully as the traditional one does, while honoring the integrity of the Jewish tradition.

It reads: "Blessed are you, Adonai, our God, ruler of the universe, who has made it possible for us to draw our son or daughter near to the Torah. Blessed are you, Adonai, who gives the Torah."

In the 1980s, my friend Rachel Cowan, who converted to Judaism as an adult, cowrote a book about interfaith marriage with her husband called *Mixed Blessings: Overcoming the Stumbling Blocks in an Interfaith Marriage*. Rachel was raised in a New England Unitarian church, and her husband, Paul, had a strong Jewish identity, although he was not from an especially religious household. In fact, Paul's family was so proud of having fully assimilated that they celebrated Christmas and Easter and not Hanukkah or Passover.

Paul wrote that when he first met Rachel, the two of them "would have bridled at the suggestion—which is a theme of this book—that differences in ethnic and religious backgrounds can become 'time bombs' in relationships, especially after children are born." However, they started to question their decision to raise their two children in what he described as a "religiously neutral household." Paul related a couple of anecdotes that made them change their mind about celebrating Christian and Jewish holidays with equal weight. They took the kids to a puppet show dramatizing the story of Purim, and when one of the characters threatened to murder all Jews, their young son threw himself into Rachel's arms, pleading, "He won't get me, will he? I'm only half Jewish!" Then their daughter asked Rachel, "Mom, would it hurt your feelings if I said I was Jewish?," an experience that our daughter almost eerily echoed when she asked it of Beth almost thirty years later.

Those two events were enough to convince the Cowans that they needed to pick a single religious identity for their children. When Rachel and Paul began speaking to other families, they found they were not alone in their complicated experience of interfaith marriage. Many had realized they had stronger feelings about their heritage than they'd thought. It's "the December dilemma," they wrote: the decision about whether to celebrate Christmas, Hanukkah, or both.

The issues that Paul and Rachel Cowan were grappling with in the 1980s have become locked in to mainstream American culture. In the last decade, 45 percent of all marriages in the U.S. were between people of different faiths. Rates of interfaith marriage among Jews have seen an especially dramatic rise. Among Jews who married in 2000 or later, 58 percent had a non-Jewish spouse in 2013.

Because of these numbers, Rabbi Danny Zemel wrote a letter to the Temple Micah community in 2009, announcing "one of the greatest personal and religious decisions I have made in my career as a rabbi": to conduct interfaith marriage ceremonies. He said he would do it for the same reason that many Jews are against interfaith marriage: because he wanted to help Judaism to flourish in America.

Some Jewish communities have decided the best way for Judaism to thrive is by becoming more purist and separatist. Rabbi Zemel takes the opposite view: that Jews need to "integrate, integrate, integrate." Sitting in his book-lined office at Temple Micah one summer afternoon, he told me that he had decided integration was his best chance of having "a vibrant voice, both as a Jew and as part of American culture. Otherwise, we Jews will just be an oddity footnote in history." In his 2009 letter, he put it this way: that the new American Judaism "will have to be as open and attractive a community as it possibly can be."

Rabbi Zemel's dedication to include non-Jews is invigorating to me. His efforts to reach across the aisle validate my own path. Interfaith families like ours may make Jewish life more complicated, but Rabbi Zemel is saying that my family is welcome—and what's more, that he sees us as thriving members of a dynamically shifting community.

Interfaith marriage in America stretches well beyond the Jewish community, of course. Along the path of my religious journey, I've talked about it with faith leaders of all stripes. When I sat down with Ginger Gaines-Cirelli, the senior pastor at Beth's church, Foundry United Methodist in downtown D.C., she said she hears about interfaith issues all the time from her congregation. Pastor Ginger and I spent several hours talking in her comfortable visiting room, decorated with her collection of religious objects from all over the world.

"I often have folks coming to me who are really trying to find a middle ground," she told me. "And I think that's one of the big opportunities and challenges, is to find a spiritual practice that doesn't feel you've just gone and picked the things that worked for you. To ground it in something that's larger than just your own preferences, in other words. To find a spiritual practice that doesn't end up in a gray, not very grounded place. There's so much richness and depth to the traditions themselves."

All those years ago, Beth hoped that by urging me to explore my faith, she would draw us closer together. There is no doubt that has been true. I have come to see the many values and ideas that unite Jews and Christians: everything from "Love thy neighbor" to an emphasis on knowing and celebrating God and to trying to live up to God's expectations by thinking of others. Judaism is the lens through which I see this path, but not in an exclusive way, because I take inspiration from the teachings of Jesus and the Christian Scriptures all the time.

We did not get here right away. Before I could embrace the more universal lessons of faith, I first needed to delve deeply into the specifics of Judaism. For a while, I found it easier to see the differences than the similarities between our religions. I also spent time trying to understand my place in the story of the Jewish people, which sometimes created a wedge between Beth and me.

"If you stop eating lobster, I'll kill you!" Beth said these words to me while we were having dinner together one night, early in my Bible study with Erica, when I was experimenting with a deeper level of religious observance. Beth was making light of it, but her words hit home. I had recently decided to stop eating pork as a nod to my faith and the kosher dietary rules. After a lifetime of not understanding why some Jews keep kosher, I had come to appreciate the idea that even eating should feel holy. The kosher rules are spelled out in Leviticus and are designed to elevate the life of the Jew at all times of the day.

Beth was letting me know that I was starting down a path that made her feel left out. If I started keeping kosher now, I would deny us a secular ritual that we shared as a family. Unlike Jews who might be tempted to experiment with different versions of their faith at various times in their life, I was married to a Christian. For me to go full kosher was a step too far. Eating lobster when we are in New England is an important ritual—some would argue that it is a spiritual experience unto itself.

There were other ways I experimented with Jewish ritual. In 2008 or so, I went through a stage of laying tefillin on my arms and forehead to pray, the way some Orthodox Jews do. The practice comes from Deuteronomy, Chapter 11, which says: "You shall love the LORD your God, therefore, and keep his charge, his decrees, his ordinances, and his commandments always. You shall put these words of mine in your heart and soul, and you shall bind them as a sign on your hand, and fix them as an emblem on your forehead."

I made a trip out to the suburbs of Washington to meet with an Orthodox rabbi, who explained that rabbis had invented tefillin so that Jews could literally fulfill the commandment. Tefillin are small boxes containing tiny parchment scrolls of biblical verses, with attached leather bindings for the arms and the fingers. The rabbi analogized it to picking up something for your wife for dinner because you love her. "In the same way, if God asks you to fulfill this commandment, you do it because you love God."

As practical as that advice seemed, it felt somewhat otherworldly when I went home, placed the box on my forehead, wrapped the leather straps around my forearm, and recited Hebrew prayers. I didn't exactly hide it from my family, but I did think it was better to do it in the bedroom when Beth was not at home, out of sight of the rest of my family. One day, though, my son opened the door and found me standing, staring out the window, and praying with the black tefillin box on my head. He looked horrified and blurted out, "Daddy, what are you doing?" If the ritual was supposed to draw me closer to God, it also had the effect of making me look strange. I'd never intended to start doing it all the time. I think Beth thought it was a bit odd, but she knew not to be alarmed about it. She could tell that I was delving into Judaism with the intensity that I tend to apply to subjects that deeply interest me.

Another of our challenges is around the subject of Jewish identity. In *Mixed Blessings,* Paul and Rachel Cowan wrote, "Time and again, we have seen that an irreducible core of Jewishness is lodged inside most Jews at the junction of ethnicity and religion. But it is often hard for them to describe it and for their gentile lovers to understand it."

That was certainly our experience. I went through a stage of wanting to explore how I fit into the great tableau of Jewish life. This led to strain with Beth, though. She thought that the focus on my identity seemed like another form of self-absorption—something that she has tried to help me overcome. She told me that this part of my Jewish study seemed to be less about getting outside of myself and becoming a better person and more about me discovering me, the Jew. It was hard to hear that. But I tried to take it on and start to ask myself bigger questions about what I believe.

Honestly, Beth sometimes feels excluded by Judaism. After all, Jews believe they are "God's chosen people" who have a privileged relationship with God. If you weren't born a Jew, you cannot belong unless you convert, and according to the Orthodox and Conservative branches of Judaism, you belong only if your mother is Jewish.

Around this time, Danny Zemel suggested that I meet his mentor and teacher, Larry Hoffman, a leading thinker on interfaith matters who teaches at the Hebrew Union College in New York and has authored dozens of books on Judaism. Rabbi Hoffman was kind enough to meet me at the Rock Center Café in the NBC building one morning when I was up in New York to fill in on the *Today* show.

I began by explaining where I was on my religious path. I told him I'd been studying the Bible and that I'd practiced laying tefillin. We had not been talking longer than ten minutes before Rabbi Hoffman interrupted me. "Let me give you some advice. You're going down a path that is not for you. You are meeting and studying with Orthodox people and going down a *halakhic* path," he said, using the Hebrew term for the corpus of Jewish law. "That is not you, and it is not your family."

When I mentioned my tension with Beth over Judaism's ethnic identity, Hoffman told me that he understood how the idea of Jews as the chosen people could be alienating for non-Jews. Some years ago he decided to use a different version of the prayer that traditionally reads, "God has chosen me from among the nations of the earth." Instead, he says something which is "less harmful" to all those who might hear it, he said.

He added that I should focus on creating *shalom bayit,* which is the Hebrew phrase that means "peace in the home." "You can affirm your Jewish identity without taking on ritual aspects that are not the essence of Judaism," Rabbi Hoffman said.

Some years later, when I met Rabbi Hoffman again, I asked whether he recalled that first conversation in the Rock Center Café. He did, and explained that he'd immediately recognized my behavior. It was not uncommon for someone like me, trying to reconnect with faith, to identify with "the more visual aspects of Jewish ritual behavior," as he put it. But those practices are not universal among Jews, and he wanted to drive home the point that they can be alienating. Judaism is meant to strengthen the family, not create gaps within it, he said.

This subject is close to Rachel Cowan's heart. When I met her in her New York apartment on a hot July day for one of our semi-regular chats about faith, she told me that she often sees religion create gaps in the home. It is a special concern among interfaith couples, she said, though it can happen between two people of the same faith if one of them is, for instance, more interested in investigating religion or a relationship with God.

She told me about a dear friend of hers, named Larry, who announced to some of his friends, "Hey, I've come out as a seeker." He was being self-deprecating with the phrase, aware that his wasn't as large a decision as the other kind of coming out. But it was hard for him to admit it and to apply the word "seeker" to himself. Rachel said she could understand that feeling. "Saying you are a seeker is going out on a limb for something you can't prove. And sometimes it is hard for your family and friends to deal with it."

Larry was having trouble praying, Rachel said, and he wanted to get better at it, so a teacher of his suggested trying out different things. "So he's sitting in bed one night, and his wife came in and said, 'What are you doing?' And he told her, 'I'm writing a letter to God.' And she was like, 'Oh no!' She was thinking, What's happening to Larry? He's getting so weird . . . where's he going to go next?" Even though Larry and his wife were both Jewish, his wife found his religious exploration destabilizing because she could not share in it.

I am lucky that Beth *does* think about God and her belief. Larry Hoffman nailed our experience on the head: "You decided to follow the Jewish map along your spiritual path. Beth may have had some concern that this map would take you on a different path altogether, and it turns out it doesn't. It turns out that it actually takes you deeper into the path that she's already on."

There's no doubt that these concerns were hard on our marriage. She never expressed any interest in studying with me, and that saddened me for a time. I know the kids can sense when we aren't on the same page about religion, and I have often wished it were otherwise.

When it came to building ritual for the family and some of the actual Jewish practice, I felt alone at times. For the most part, religious ritual is something Beth neither is inclined to do nor has time for right now. It's also not something that she feels she needs to do; she is not a seeker, like me. She grew up grounded in her faith, and that is part of who she is now.

Beth was more invested in some of the rituals than others. Our weekly Shabbat dinner was one that she wanted to apply herself to. On Fridays, Beth lights the candles; she breaks the bread and says the prayers. Our Shabbat ritual feels as much hers as mine, a melding of her Sunday Sabbath with my Jewishness. She likes to make sure that non-Jews attend our Shabbat dinners, and she emphasizes the similarity of this ritual to the Christian Sunday Sabbath she grew up with.

Beth is stalwart about steering our religious obser vance toward a universal language of faith, and she is a steadying force in our religious lives. She makes sure the kids go to Sunday school. She has taken the lead in organizing Max's bar mitzvah. Even if Beth is not on the same journey that I am, she is proud of having been the guiding hand in my decision to deepen my faith, and she welcomes my efforts to do so.

Beth and I have learned a great deal about our religious lives in recent years. I can't say that always feels like a blessing, but when I stand back to get perspective, I do believe it is. That October day we sat out on the patio together, I asked her a question I'd never asked her outright: "When you think about the influence that you have, and are having, on my and the kids' spiritual lives, does it feel like it is worth it to have given up raising them Christian?"

Her answer was yes at first, but she quickly tempered it. "I think it's worth it for you and the kids . . . I mean, we may never know. I don't know whether they would have felt a deeper connection to Christianity if they had been raised in the church rather than as Jews. I just don't know."

Because the kids have not especially taken to Hebrew school, Beth recently initiated the question of whether Christianity might be easier for kids to access. When Beth sees them struggling with Hebrew, she wonders whether the language presents too much of a barrier.

I have to agree that the Jewish education system is flawed, and the problem extends beyond the day-of-the-week issue. Judaism doesn't have a single textbook. Using the Torah to teach ethics would be like trying to teach people about America by having them read the Constitution when they've never gone to a baseball game, as Rabbi Zemel puts it.

Beth thinks that it will be a hard road for the kids to find a spiritual center in Judaism. She may be right. They are comfortable enough in our rituals, but they aren't especially engaged. Of course, that may be their ages, but Beth worries that they engage even less because she does not share their religion. For instance, she doesn't feel comfortable playing an active role in our synagogue, whereas if we attended church every week as a family, she would want to be a church usher. She imagines that she would talk to the kids about the sermon after church, as her mom did with her.

Also, Judaism is more abstract and intangible than

Christianity. When you walk into a church, the primary worship symbol of the cross is right there on the wall. In Catholic and Anglican churches, you partake of God's body and blood through the wafer and the wine. There is nothing like that direct interaction in Jewish practice. During services, the rabbi will ceremoniously remove the Torah from the ark and walk through the congregation holding this symbol of the Jewish faith. Sometimes worshippers will kiss the Torah as the rabbi passes by. But even this symbol is more abstract than the body of Christ, since the Torah represents the word of God.

I find it deeply fulfilling to consider the words of God. But my children do not, and perhaps they never will. I have to acknowledge that it is possible they will not share what I love about Judaism and Jewish identity. I am trying to come to terms with the fact that by making the choice we did, Beth and I may have made it harder for our kids to develop a robust spiritual life. I do believe our kids are lucky to have two parents with a deep faith. I can only hope that something of this will filter down.

Once, after I gave a speech to a Jewish federation, someone asked me how to talk to your children about the importance of being a Jew. My answer was "Say nothing. Do something." As Jonathan Sacks, the former chief rabbi of the United Hebrew Congregations of the Commonwealth, wrote in his book *A Letter in the Scroll*: "You cannot command that your children be Jews. You can only lead a beautiful life and hope they see it as beautiful too."

•   •   •

The bells were ringing all up and down Sixteenth Street in Washington, D.C. It was a sunny fall Sunday morning in 2014, one of those days when the weather has just started to sharpen and the air feels fresh. All up and down the wide thoroughfare, the doors of different churches were open, and there was nowhere to park for many blocks around.

Beth and I had decided to come to Foundry United Methodist Church, her church home in Washington. She feels she doesn't attend services often enough, and I had recently resolved to start going to church with her more frequently—once a month, perhaps—because I knew she would enjoy it more with me than alone. The kids were at our synagogue for Hebrew school, as they often are on Sunday morning.

I decided to wear a suit, which was not strictly necessary, but it gives Beth pleasure to dress up for church. She was wearing a lovely peach-colored dress, and I could tell she was happy: The sun was shining brightly, and here I was at church with her for the first time in years.

We got there a little early so that Beth could enjoy the church bells. She teared up the moment she heard them, and I sat beside her in the pew, holding her hand. Several church volunteers approached us before the service began, including the church's executive pastor. We were struck by that friendly and welcoming gesture, a marked difference from some of the synagogues we have attended together.

Foundry has high ceilings, but its dome is painted

white, giving it a bright, open, and modern feel, appropriate for its mission. Foundry describes itself as both "historic" and "progressive." The service we attended relied heavily on the organ and a traditional red-and-white-robed choir to lead us through the hymns from the Methodist hymnal. But the clergy is racially diverse, and its senior pastor is one of a minority of female pastors in the Methodist Church.

At the beginning of the service, one of the church leaders called a group of children to stand in front of the choir. A leader asked them to answer the question "What is love?," and they started throwing out answers. "Passion," said one. "Dedication" and "Friends and family," came the responses. What a great way to begin a religious service, I thought, with a callout to love.

As we drove to pick up the kids from Hebrew school, Beth and I talked about Pastor Ginger's sermon, which was called "Loving Matters." In it, she made the point that Jesus interprets the law through love: "Jesus' love is the key that sets us free, that opens the door to life in God's Kingdom." Now, Beth and I may think of Jesus differently, but we both responded to that message.

We also liked how Pastor Ginger spoke of "being and becoming who God created me to be." Beth said that it made her think about the idea that we are all always in transition. Some of us may be in a more obvious transition—as I am, on my faith journey—but Beth, too, is constantly shifting. She talked about how, when she makes church part of the rhythm of her week, it helps her assess and reflect on her life in a way she has trouble doing otherwise. "Being and becoming" also speaks to how often I feel I am falling short of my spiritual goal to become the person God expects me to be.

I told her that if she wanted to bring the kids to church sometimes, she should do that. We had been worried about confusing them, but they were older now—anyway, I said, it was worth it, if for no other reason than to have them support their mom. She smiled gratefully.

Perhaps Christians and Jews are on the same path, just with different maps. We find ourselves side by side with our maps, circling each other. We are, as Larry Hoffman put it, "a double helix. The two sides never collapse into one another." I love that image: a double helix spiraling around, sometimes mirroring each other but never touching.

Passover is a great example of that. I think it is the most accessible and universal of all the stories in the Jewish tradition. Like Easter, it is a springtime renewal. And while it commemorates a very powerful moment of Jewish peoplehood—the exodus of the Israelites from Egyptian slavery—Passover is also a call to broader humanity. Every year, Jews "relive slavery and indignity and then we re-experience the exhilarating gift of divine liberation," according to the *Haggadah*, the book that helps explain the seder meal, the main event of Passover.

Though Beth misses sharing the uplifting message of Easter with our kids, she likes Passover more than any other Jewish holiday. Some years ago, I decided to try a family play on Passover in an effort to get the kids excited about the holiday. We act out the story before the meal, and while I would love to make it elaborate, I've learned that we are most successful if we keep it short. We start out the night in our front room, lighting the candles and singing songs like the African-American spiritual "Go Down Moses":

When Israel was in Egypt's land
Let my people go.
Oppressed so hard they could not stand
Let my people go.
Go down, Moses,
Way down in Egypt's land,
Tell old Pharaoh,
Let my people go.

I write up a different script for the play each year, some more successful than others. We all don costumes. I play the part of the adult Moses, long white hair, beard, brown robe, and all. The part of Baby Moses has been played by anyone we can fit in a laundry basket: Jed and Ava have each taken on the role, and so has Gus, our dog. For Passover 2014, I wrote a script with a Twitter theme—what better way to keep it short?—which gave Max the opportunity to deliver the memorable line: "#IdontrememberMosesbeingadog."

The story of Jewish liberation is an essential part of Jewish identity. We are reminded in the Bible to "love the stranger as yourself" because we were once strangers in the land of Egypt. We were once slaves, and then we were freed—that should be a lesson that directs how we live in the world and treat others.

Sometimes I'll put cards under the dinner plates on

Passover with questions like "What is an example of a modern-day slavery or plague?" or "Is it ever justified to kill someone as God kills Pharaoh's son?" We'll have a discussion with the kids about the universal truths that Passover reminds us of: We should welcome the stranger and the poor into our home. We should be committed to justice. We should use our experience to be better people in the world.

I've changed how I think about my faith as I have progressed in my learning. Initially, I felt a great pull toward the insularity of my Jewishness. But at some point, I got to a place where I was able to separate my ethnic Jewish identity from my spiritual identity. I began to believe that it does not necessarily dilute my religious experience if I focus on the aspects of Judaism that are more universal.

Once I set off to look for commonality with my wife's beliefs, I realized that I wanted to think about the values and purpose of my religion in a larger way. The same ethics, the same Scripture, the same stories can hold great meaning for all of us. Increasingly, I have found myself experiencing moments of universality within my Judaism. I had a moment of epiphany during the long and solemn Yom Kippur service one recent year, when Rabbi Zemel was reciting "*Unetanneh Tokef,*" a poem that is part of the liturgy: "This is Your glory: You are slow to anger, ready to forgive. It is not the death of sinners You seek, but that they should turn from their ways and live. Until the last day You wait for them, welcoming them as soon as they turn to You."

I have heard the poem many times during Yom Kippur services. But it struck me that this moment was really about salvation; that Yom Kippur is a rehearsal of death, and as we take stock of our lives, we acknowledge that we will stand before God, the King, and be judged. I leaned in to Beth, sitting beside me in the pew, and whispered, "Jews may not like to talk about God in general, but this poem is exactly what Christians do. Here, Jews are turning to God and asking to be inscribed in the book of life."

In the Christian tradition, the worshipper comes before God, penitent. William Sloane Coffin, the progressive Christian thinker who served as the pastor of New York's Riverside Church for many years, said it this way: "If we are not yet one in life, at least we are one in sin, which is no mean bond because it preludes the possibility of separation through judgment."

In other words, we humans are united by our sin and by the need for salvation. This very Jewish poem, "*Unetanneh Tokef*," has much the same message. We are repenting. We are asking God to save us.

In recent years, my journey has become less of a Jewish pilgrimage and more that of a religious pilgrim investigating the different faces of God. Nevertheless, I have tried to be specific. I approach many different religious leaders for their counsel, but when it comes to belief and identity, being Jewish is enough for me. I don't want to become a half Christian or a half Buddhist. I just want to see and understand other ways of believing, in the hope that it will help me forge a greater connection to God and thicken my personal relationships.

I think it is fair to say we are all on a spiritual journey to God—we are born into a tradition, choose a tradition, or choose not to believe. Larry Hoffman likes to say that each faith has a room in what he calls a "museum of the human spirit." We share a room with our own people, Lutherans or Catholics or Muslims, all of us working away at our life projects, constantly renovating.

From time to time, we wander into other rooms in this faith museum. That doesn't mean we are turning our back on our room, Hoffman says; but after visiting another room, we can't help being changed. We might return to our own room and find our practice enlivened and deepened. We might even find ourselves shifting in another direction for a while. But we are all part of the same project—the project of the human spirit.

CHAPTER 6

Humility

Who Would You Be if You Lost Your Job?

———————✳———————

How do you tell your children you've lost your job? That's a question I asked myself many times after things began to get bad with NBC in the spring and summer of 2014.

First some background. Let's start with inauguration weekend, 2009. Barack Obama was about to be sworn in as America's first black president, and Washington was bustling with preparations and parties. On *Meet the Press* that Sunday, I talked to President-elect Obama's incoming chief of staff, Rahm Emanuel, about the big challenges Obama had inherited—economic turmoil and a multifront war on terror. And then I brought in a political round table to discuss whether President Obama would be able to live up to the high expectations.

It was a fun time to be settling into my new role. I'd just come on as moderator six weeks prior, and there was a satisfying symmetry to starting my new role while a new president was being sworn in, especially because I had covered the White House throughout Bush's eight-year tenure.

After the show, Beth and I went down to an inauguration brunch that MSNBC was throwing near the White House. As we walked to the event, a couple of people leaned out of a car and yelled at me on the street, "Hey, David, love you! Love watching the show! Congratulations!" I waved back, feeling grateful if somewhat self-conscious about the new level of attention I was receiving. For her part, Beth found it hilarious. She couldn't help but poke a little fun at me. She looked at me and said sarcastically, "Wow, it's amazing how much better-looking and popular you've become since you got the job."

"And how much of a better journalist!" I added, laughing.

Moderator of *Meet the Press* was a lofty perch to occupy, at a difficult time to take it on. I was succeeding Tim Russert, a man beloved by America. Because of his stature, there had been a great deal of intrigue about who would follow Tim on the show. Tom Brokaw even made an allusion to that at Tim's memorial service at the Kennedy Center in June 2008, when fifteen hundred people gathered to say goodbye. In his opening tribute, Tom said that the assembled crowd included family, friends, "and the largest group—those who think they should be his successor on *Meet the Press*." That got a big laugh.

I came into the job feeling plenty of pressure to live

up to the standard Tim had set for the show. I was euphoric about the opportunity and excited about what I could do with the show. I was also aware that the effusive attention was a benefit that came with the job. That was why Beth and I laughed as we walked to the brunch that inauguration weekend: Yes, I had been given this platform, but it was important to remember that in no way did that mean I was now the smartest journalist in Washington or the most destined to succeed. I'd covered Washington and graduated to this position. Beth and I vowed to enjoy the ride, however long it lasted.

This was where my faith helped me. Being on a more spiritual path gave me a little bit of perspective. It made me feel more grounded, understanding that the job wasn't everything and that there would be lots of highs and lows. So while I did not at all mind that people were shouting my name enthusiastically and saying nice things about me, I knew better than to get carried away by it all.

I also knew that my task—to succeed Tim so soon after his untimely death—was daunting. It's like what Russell Baker said when asked if he'd like to succeed the venerable Alistair Cooke as host of the PBS show *Masterpiece Theatre:* "I'd like to be the man who succeeds the man who succeeds Alistair Cooke." I would need to work hard to do justice to the longest-running program in American television history.

Before my first show, Jeff Zucker, then the president and CEO of NBC Universal, invited me to lunch with several others at the highest levels of the company. It was to be a big embrace, a way of saying, "We've chosen you to succeed Tim at this tough time: Now go forth and conquer." Zucker took me up a back staircase to the fifty-third floor of 30 Rockefeller Plaza, the building that houses NBC and its former parent, GE. Inside a private room, he brought me to GE CEO Jeffrey Immelt, who asked me, "So how are you thinking about all this?"

I said, "Well, I'm pretty scared."

He said, "Good. You should be. *Meet the Press* is a show I watch." He encouraged me to be who I am and to create my own identity for the program, suggesting that they knew it would not be easy, but they were behind me.

That was a refrain I heard often in the early days of my tenure: It was important to make the show my own, but to do so slowly. Clearly, Tim had a successful formula. It was a slow build for me, establishing my identity as moderator. At first I focused my energies on making sure the audience trusted me, and to living up to the gravitas and objectivity that we all admired Tim for. I was working with Tim's longtime producer, Betsy Fischer, and we decided not to overhaul anything. We did not change the set or modify the theme music for the first two years I was on *Meet the Press*.

I remember a woman approaching me on the street about a year into my tenure and saying, "I was a huge fan of Tim. I loved Tim. I wasn't so sure about you, but as I've watched you, I've come to think you're doing a good job." One woman told me that she thought I had grown in the job. That kind of viewer feedback meant a great deal to me, because it felt genuine, and I had worked hard for it. Within NBC, I was trying to prove myself as a leader of the *Meet the Press* crew and staff, to mature into the new role in which I had more leadership. For the first three years I moderated the show, *Meet the Press* remained in first place among the Sunday news programs.

Right from the start, it was the greatest job I ever had. It was high-impact journalism; viewers paid close attention to the interviews. I loved the chance to talk to people in long form, and the opportunity to hold leaders accountable for their decisions and policies. The show also gave me a unique ability to build up some expertise on stories over a period of months.

Our spring 2012 interview with Vice President Joe Biden was an example of that. For many months beforehand, I had been working with my producer, Chris Donovan, to prep questions about gay marriage. We knew the administration was going to change its position at some point. Chris researched and briefed me on it all the time. But we actually had not planned to ask Biden about it. With Biden, there were endless ways to make news. He's an old-fashioned pol who talks a lot and freely. I had a list of questions about the economy and the election that I wanted to get through. On my outline, I had scrawled "gay marriage" in a bottom corner just in case it came up.

As it happened, during the taping, Biden gave me an opening I did not want to pass up. He quoted his grandfather Finnegan as saying that the Republican Party needed a better social policy.

"You raise social policy," I said. "I'm curious. You know, the president has said that his views on gay marriage, on same-sex marriage, have evolved. But he's opposed to it. You're opposed to it. Have your views . . . evolved?"

He hedged a little, but after I continued to press him, he answered, "I am absolutely comfortable with the fact that men marrying men, women marrying women, and heterosexual men and women marrying another are entitled to the same exact rights, all the civil rights, all the civil liberties. And quite frankly, I don't see much of a distinction—beyond that." Then he said that the TV show *Will & Grace* "probably did more to educate the American public than almost anything anybody's ever done so far." I thought, Whoa, I think we are headed to news-making land here!

After the taping, Biden hung around chatting, and on the sidelines, I asked Chris what he thought. "Oh my God, he just totally changed the position on gay marriage," he said.

This was Thursday, so the interview was not set to air for a few more days. During that time, the White House kept insisting that it had not changed its policy on gay marriage. But I heard from someone at the White House that Dan Pfeiffer, President Obama's senior communications adviser, was reading through the transcript on the Thursday we taped, and screamed out in horror, "Will and fucking Grace?"

After the interview aired, it became a huge story: Biden had effectively backed same-sex marriage. On Monday morning, the story was on the front page of *The New York Times*. Three days later, President Obama announced that he had been "going through an evolution" on the issue of gay marriage, and if he were governor of a state, he would vote in favor.

When I was a student at American University, *Nightline*'s Ted Koppel came to speak on a panel discussion. At the reception afterward, I asked him for advice, and he told me: "It's really important to listen closely during an interview." I thought about that when I started at *Meet the Press,* and I thought about it as I talked to Joe Biden that day.

That was the show at its best, setting the standard for news and driving it through the cycle. It was also an increasingly rare occurrence. Politicians have become so much more scripted on these shows. Biden was an exception, which was also why he never returned to our set—though, believe me, we asked.

Six years after I became moderator of *Meet the Press,* I was facing the lowest moment of my professional career. I was about to leave the network for good.

The ratings had been slipping at *Meet the Press,* and I had a new boss at NBC News, Deborah Turness, who was pushing us hard to reimagine the show. Some of her ideas were pretty unorthodox. I had been trying new ideas at the show well before she came on board, but I thought it was essential that we retain the qualities of the program that had made it popular for so long.

Other elements were shifting, too. The TV landscape had changed. NBC and its parent company, Comcast, had seen sliding ratings on *Today* as well as *Nightly News.*

The Sunday shows were struggling to retain their place as appointment viewing. Booking guests whom viewers really wanted to see had become more difficult.

By the time I made the announcement that I was leaving *Meet the Press* in August 2014, NBC and I had been in discussions for several weeks. I didn't want to leave, but I was not happy. I was getting a lot of bad press about falling ratings, and many of the stories speculated on whether I would be replaced. It was frustrating, because I knew that people within NBC were leaking stories—saying I was about to be pushed out, in order to weaken my position, even as my bosses were telling me that was not the case. The press coverage seemed excessively personal, as though I had done something wrong.

That summer I decided to stay above the fray—I didn't talk to reporters, either privately or publicly, to defend myself or to tell them what was going on behind the scenes. But I needed the network to stand behind me. I knew Washington and politics. Now that there was blood in the water, it would only get worse. I told my bosses that the attention was becoming too much about me. It was bad for the show and for what we were trying to do.

My relationship with *Meet the Press* during that last year was like a marriage that you know is bad but you can't leave. I was miserable, but I needed to be told the company didn't support me before I could come to terms with the end. Although NBC backed me initially, the network decided late in the summer that it would not commit to me in the long term. Clearly, that was the signal that it was time to go. Could I have done something else at the network? In theory, yes. But as the damaging leaks kept coming, it became clear to me that they weren't interested in that. It never came up as an option.

The last gasp came suddenly, and the timing was bad: Beth and I were setting off on a day of travel to pick up our kids from camp in New Hampshire. Just before the plane doors closed and I had to power down my phone, my agent called to tell me that NBC had decided it didn't want to risk another "Ann Curry moment," which has become a byword in the TV business for an on-air embarrassment, after Curry's long and tearful farewell from her job as *Today* show cohost. Because of this ill-conceived concern, NBC decided not to let me have a final show. They wanted this to be my last day. I was furious when I heard that. I felt like they were snuffing me out.

As Beth drove our rental car through the bucolic New England farmlands, I couldn't stop thinking about how much I wanted to be able to say goodbye to the *Meet the Press* viewers. I had one of my first friends in TV news on my mind. Nolan Snook was a salesman for a station I worked at in Albuquerque, New Mexico. He had a memorable shock of white hair, and he had come from big-market television, so he knew the ropes. He told me that jobs in the news business are fleeting. "Just remember, David," he told me, "they've given you a forum. Everything you have in your relationship with the public is based on this forum. And they can take it away at any time."

I was not going to be able to control the messaging. My cell signal kept going in and out after we turned off the interstate and onto a country road, and at some point along Route 104, I saw on my Twitter feed that NBC had leaked that I was out at *Meet the Press*.

This goodbye was never going to be easy. I'd been working in TV news since I was eighteen. Since I graduated from school, I had rarely been off the air longer than a week, other than vacations. I worked every summer during college, and I got my first job, in Albuquerque, before I graduated. I had my sights set solidly on a job at the network for eight years until I got it, and I had planned each stage of the journey I'd take to get there. After that, it was a new set of goals. And *Meet the Press* was a destination that had exceeded my expectations.

After a career spent entirely in TV news, I had come to rely on being on the air. It was my way to measure how good a week I had. Other people assess their professional achievements through meetings attended, classes taught, or surgical operations conducted; for me, it's always been about airtime. When I was a reporter, being on the air a lot was shorthand for being in the middle of covering a big story. The equivalent at *Meet the Press* was how well spent my hourlong show was each week, and how much pickup the interviews got. Now, in the middle of my life, I would have to completely recalibrate my ideas about productivity and worth.

Sitting in the car that day, watching the tweets stack up about my rumored departure, I was far from at peace with all of it. I had spent so much time planning out my career. It hurt to see how far out of my control this ending was. There was also the feeling that I'd be seen as a failure. I'd had a big setback, and everyone was going to know it.

It was one of these moments people talk about: Something bad is happening to you, and you are watching yourself in slow motion from the outside. I had feared this moment would come. As the ratings slid and the press got worse, I had played out the scenario in my head. Now it was real. And one of the things I was conscious of was that I should handle it well.

I was thinking about the question that Erica once asked me: "Who would you be if you lost it all?" When she asked, I was so attached to my position—and the influence that accompanied it—that it was hard to imagine feeling that my life had purpose without the job. But I'd had six years to contemplate the answer to the question, so I was prepared, at least in this way: I had come to believe that my job was not my entire identity. I felt fuller than that.

I took a deep breath and made a point of considering the ways my life would not change. I was a lucky guy. I might be losing my job, but unlike a lot of people in this position, I had enough money, and my wife would remain a senior partner at a big law firm. This loss hurt, but it was not a crisis that would undermine our ability to take care of our children.

As we drove, Beth reached out and touched my knee. She cried a bit, seeing how upset I was. It was always going to hurt when the ending became official and public, she reminded me. Still, this had hit her harder than I'd expected it would. Beth is the steely one. "Scrutiny is part of the job and merely the flip side to the positive feedback you get," she would always say. Often she'd joke that no one walked up to her on the street to tell her they loved her work as a lawyer. "Keep your head down and do the job" was her frequent counsel.

This was different, though. Beth could see that it was not a matter of my ego. She thought that NBC had left me to twist in the wind; the long and public nature of my departure seemed unnecessary. As we reached the final leg of the drive, she pulled over so we could collect ourselves before seeing the kids. She hugged me and told me that she was proud of me for how I was handling myself.

Then we drove in to Camp Merrowvista. The campers' duffel bags were lined up in tidy piles on one side of the grass field serving as a parking lot. There were signs directing parents to pick up their kids on the playground. I was eager to reunite with our kids, but I wanted to issue a public statement as quickly as I could, before an official statement came from NBC. Before I did that, I had to call my agent and others. I asked the camp office to loan me a phone, since I still had no cell signal, and they offered me a spare office.

Hanging up the phone, I heard the kids screaming and laughing outside, and I realized that I couldn't ask for a better way to experience this low moment in my career. Being so far from the Washington and New York media circus made it easier to start letting go. My world was about to explode all over social media, but I was free to enjoy my more serene surroundings. After twenty years as a fairly hard-driving, ambitious, and competitive journalist, I was about to experience a change. Who knew what would happen next.

I set off to find Max and Ava, who were hanging out in one of the cabins. I gave them big hugs, and Max didn't waste any time in asking how our team had done in the Little League World Series qualifying tournament that summer. It had been killing him not to know; they are cut off from the Internet up at camp. At the age of twelve, Max has every intention of playing basketball or baseball at the college level. Nothing matters as much as his teams.

I had to break the bad news that the team had lost. A setback, but next summer would be Max's opportunity to compete on the team, so, like a presidential candidate eyeing the next cycle he was already making plans to succeed where others had fallen short. I was pleased that I'd remembered to check the score, but for Max, that was not enough. He wanted details, like who was pitching and whether there had been any home runs. As his briefer, I was never prepared enough to satisfy my son's demands.

Then I found Jed, playing Frisbee on the basketball court with some other kids, and he jumped into my arms. I told them I would join them at dinner before the Grand Council Meeting, the final event of camp.

Walking back up to the office, I thought about how I would explain to the kids what had happened. I would need to do it pretty quickly. Once we got back to Washington and they returned to school, someone was likely to talk, and they could explore for themselves what people had written about me. I wanted to be the one to tell them, I just wasn't sure *how* I would break the news. Part of my reluctance was plain embarrassment. The kids were old enough to worry about me, and that wasn't a good feeling. But I also knew that this was the kind of moment when I could teach my otherwise pampered children that setbacks happen and you have to persevere.

I was thinking about them, and about how I wanted to handle myself when a lot of people were paying attention as I sat down to write the words that would make it official on Twitter. To the degree that I had thought about losing my job, I had not envisioned myself sitting alone on a campground in the mountains of New Hampshire, sending out a forty-seven-word announcement. But I specifically remember thinking, Here's my chance. This was a moment to ask myself what God expected of me, and to act in a way that would serve as a model for my kids. Though I was alone I felt that I was being watched, in a larger way. I wrote: "I leave NBC as I came—humbled and grateful. I love journalism and serving as moderator of MTP was the highest honor there is. I have great respect for my colleagues at NBC News and wish them all well. To the viewers, I say thank you."

Okay, so it was a tweet. I don't want to blow it out of proportion; it wasn't the most profound thing anyone has ever said. But in a way, the experience did feel profound. With those few words, I felt like I was able to publicly transcend the bitterness I was feeling. (Still, I don't want to sound like a martyr here: Clearly, I would rather not have had the experience at all.)

Moments afterward, NBC issued its press release announcing my replacement. I called my executive producer from the camp phone and asked him to gather the *Meet the Press* staff so I could say goodbye to them all on speakerphone. It was important to me that they heard from me right away. I wanted to thank them and to apologize for how it was ending. I told them that I was proud of what we'd done and urged them to continue doing their best work.

Supportive messages and calls began coming in, from colleagues like *Today* show coanchor Matt Lauer and Phil Griffin, my best friend at NBC, a thirty-year veteran of the network who is now the president of MSNBC. Jamie Dimon, the CEO of J. P. Morgan, called right away—and this is a guy with throat cancer—to say: "The people who respected you before will respect you now."

As gratifying as it was to receive these messages shoring me up, I could hear that the Grand Council Meeting was about to start, so I shut the door to the office and left the Twitter stream behind. My phone battery was now dead; I was completely cut off for the next couple of hours.

My wife and the kids were sitting on the grass, holding paper plates of salad and pasta. When I sat down with them, Beth gave me a big hug. We didn't talk about it—now was not the time—but Jed must have been able to tell that something was going on: He presented me with a big soothing M&M's cookie from the buffet. I felt a dizzying mix of emotions: sad and distressed but also proud of myself, and perhaps most of all, happy to be able to walk away from the drama and relax with my family. Here were the two things that mattered to me most: my work and my family. One door had just closed, but my family life was stronger than ever.

Beth and I and the other parents gathered around the firepit and watched the campers excitedly file onto the stage for their final celebration. It was a slightly out-of-body experience, to disappear into the narrow and consuming world of my kids' camp at the end of a day I could not forget if I wanted to. But it also felt good not to have to talk or think about it all, and I was grateful for the time to let my emotions simmer down.

Sitting there on a rough bench on the side of a hill in New Hampshire, I found myself paying special attention to the camp director's speech. He referred to the camp motto: "My own self, at my very best, all the time." I was struck at that moment by how much those words meant to me. Just as I hoped my kids were growing and maturing through the Camp Merrowvista experience, so was I. I had spent months struggling to be my own self in my work by steering *Meet the Press* in the way I thought best. I'd had to battle different personalities at the network, and it had been a challenge to be my best self when it mattered most.

Now I felt angry, wronged, embarrassed. But what was the camp director telling these kids—and all of us parents—about personal growth? That we have to re-mind ourselves to find the way to be our best selves every day. That this is hard work and it doesn't stop. That summer, Max had fought with a kid in his cabin, but the two of them had learned to get along, even if they were not going to be the best of friends.

As the smoke rose into the clear summer sky, I felt almost as though the camp director were preaching to me. As hellish as the day had been, I hoped that the final battle with NBC represented my becoming the best I could be. I had tried to be my best self in a bad situation. I would leave this New Hampshire hillside having reclaimed my children—and a piece of myself.

It was all coming together: Here was the time for me to live out so many of the lessons I'd been learning on my spiritual journey. I'd been contemplating living a more spiritual, meaningful existence, and now was the time to walk the walk. In a way, that day up in New Hampshire clarified many of the discoveries I had been making about life and faith.

It is our job in the world to strive to be our best self all the time. But the time when it matters most is when things are hard. That is the true test of our character. In the months since I left NBC, I've come to a conclusion: If I do not change as a result of this experience, then it was not worth it. That's not to say the way that I left was my choice. But it happened as it happened, and I am determined to be the better for it.

One day, as the long, drawn-out drama of my departure from NBC was coming to a head, I met the Southern Baptist leader Russell Moore at his Capitol Hill office. It was already feeling inevitable that I would leave, and

Erica's question "Who would you be?" was weighing on my mind. I asked Dr. Moore how he would answer someone who came to him asking, "Who does God expect me to be?"

Dr. Moore answered me with his own questions. "The fundamental question here is 'Who are you?'" he said. "Whether you have a national profile, or you are the guy running a hardware store in a small town, you are ultimately facing the same question, which is: Do you define yourself by your work or as someone created in the image of God? Are you the owner of the hardware store or someone who must give an account to God?"

He quoted Matthew 26, in which one of Jesus' followers lashes out at the men who come to arrest him, cutting off one man's ear with a sword. "Put your sword back into its place," Jesus tells his follower. "For all who take the sword will perish by the sword."

Dr. Moore said that one of the ways he likes to interpret that Scripture is in terms of ambition. Jesus was reminding his follower that kindness and humanity matter above all. Anyone who views himself primarily in terms of ambition can start to dehumanize, "to become the sort of person who claws and fights to keep what they want," he said.

Those words held some truth for me. It's no secret that TV news is a rough business. And I'm as guilty as the rest of putting myself first on the route to the top. I'm a product of it—TV news is the only industry I have ever been a part of, other than the hospitality industry, if you count working at a restaurant in high school. My effort to rise above the rancor of the TV business has been a long, shaky process. I think sometimes about a day during my final spring at NBC when Erica came over to study with me in my office at *Meet the Press*.

She overheard me on the phone, complaining about a lack of support from my bosses, and when I hung up, she said, "David, you are using all these warlike themes in your speech." Defensively, I said something like "Well, they're going after me, what else can I do?" But as I thought through the conversation I'd just had, I realized I had said, "I may be bloodied, but I'm still standing" and "I just gotta hunker down and get through this." She was right: Many of my instincts are from the survival bunker.

"I don't hear you using the language of love," Erica said. It seemed almost laughable to me then, the idea of speaking the language of love when I was being made a target by the press and undermined by superiors who seemed to have only a tepid interest in dealing with the problems at the show. But then Erica quoted Proverbs 4:26: "Consider the path of your feet, and all your paths will be established."

I did not know right away what she meant by those words, but we really studied them that afternoon and considered their meaning. If you're inside a maze on the ground floor, Erica told me, you have a single perspective. But if you can climb up to the balcony, you can see much more; you can figure out where you're headed.

Later, she told me that what she wanted to help me do was "create the habits and language of mindfulness. Then you will have that language, even when others are speaking to you using a different vocabulary, of mean-ness." She reminded me that I should try to speak my new spiritual language all the time, not just at home, when I feel like being the good dad and making pancakes for the kids. With my colleagues and my boss, too.

"Consider the path of your feet, and all your paths will be established." Your feet must be pointed in the right direction at all times. I printed out those words and kept them on my desktop computer at NBC as a reminder throughout the last months.

The night when we picked up the kids from camp in New Hampshire, we all stayed at an inn in the town of Tuftonboro. In the morning, Beth went down to the lobby before the rest of us, and she overheard some peo-ple talking about how I had lost my job the previous day. She went over and very politely informed them that they were talking about her husband. "We haven't told our kids yet," she said. "So if you wouldn't mind keeping your voices down when you are talking about that . . ."

They were very apologetic, she said. I know Beth was feeling protective of me in the moment, but she was especially worried about the kids. She and I had talked about how I should break the news to them, and we'd decided that I should do it as soon as I could, but also casually, so as not to make it into a big deal.

To get to the airport in Manchester, we wanted to take a slightly longer route along the prettier back roads. To make sure we had enough time, I had to rush Max out of the café where we had breakfast before he was able to finish his crepes. He was a little cranky about that and, like the other two, antsy about a day of travel before getting home. We piled into the rental car, where they were cramped and uncomfortable. They started talking over one another and accusing one another of interrupting. "They were so sweet to each other yesterday at camp!" I said wistfully to Beth. "What happened?"

Amid all the bickering, my cell phone rang, and I could see it was Matt Lauer. He'd left a message the day before and had said he would try me again, but I was surprised by his persistence. I asked the kids to pipe down, as I had an important call. On the phone, Matt was very gracious. He told me he felt bad about what happened, and he had every confidence that I'd be successful in whatever I did next. Later on, both the chairman of NBC, Steve Burke, and the CEO of Comcast, Brian Roberts, reached out to me. For that I will always be grateful.

Before I hung up with Matt, I said that it meant a great deal to me that he had gotten ahold of me right away. We'd never been close; I'd found him hard to get to know. But that made it even classier that he'd reached out to me.

"Who was that, Dad?" Max asked from the backseat when I put my phone down.

I shot Beth a look and then caught Max's eye in the rearview mirror and said, "Matt Lauer."

Max knew exactly whom I meant. He is a fan of the *Today* show and would often inform me that it was more interesting than *Meet the Press*. "Why was *he* calling you?" Max said.

I took a breath and looked straight ahead as I told

them that he was calling because I was leaving NBC. "I'm no longer going to be doing *Meet the Press,*" I announced.

They all looked surprised, which is not especially easy to achieve with our world-wise kids. Max spoke up first with a down-to-business question. "Do we have to sell our house?"

I explained that we'd been very fortunate, and had been smart about saving our money, so we didn't need to worry about that.

Then Ava asked, "Did you get fired?"

I had not entirely decided how I wanted to answer that question. I should have known I'd need an answer, because Ava is a straight shooter, and there is no getting anything past her. I wanted to tell the kids what had actually happened without sugarcoating it. But I was aware that in a child's mind, people get fired because they are in the wrong, and I needed to make it clear that was not the case with me.

So I said, "Well, not exactly. We agreed that I should leave. Not because I did anything wrong, but because they wanted someone else to do the job."

They absorbed that information in silence. I think they were taking in the magnitude of it and were also unsure how to respond appropriately. I wanted to seize the moment to get across the most important point. So I continued, "You guys have seen some of the good parts of my job and me being well known, how people want my autograph or my picture. There is another side, too. People criticize me in public and write some negative things about me.

"But the big thing is I want you all to learn that not everything works out the way you planned. That's what has happened to me. But you have to persevere."

At some point later, Jed asked, "Did they make fun of you, Daddy?"

"Yes, they did," I answered, grateful that I could look straight ahead on the highway rather than having to meet his eye.

As is so often the case with kids, I couldn't tell how much my news affected them. I was glad I had been able to tell them immediately, without having to make a big deal out of it in a formal sit-down conversation.

Just a little while later, Ava and her brothers were fighting again, which I took as a sign that they were not overly traumatized by my news. Beth and I told Ava to cool it, and she leaned in toward us, chin protruding with the strength of her grievance. "But it's really hard for me to keep my self-control when they're saying mean things about me!"

It was all I could do not to laugh. "Oh, yes, it's hard," I told her. "It definitely is hard. But you can do it. Ask me how I know."

Leaving my job at NBC was a humbling experience. It was good for me—I mean it. I have to laugh about how the hits keep on coming: for instance, the people who have come up to me in the months since I have been off the show, to tell me that they love me on *Meet the Press* and never miss a single week. It's all I can do not to blurt out, "Well, you can't love me *that* much if you haven't noticed I've been gone for months now!"

My departure from NBC made for some awkward interactions initially. Often I'd be playing a guessing game, trying to work out whether someone knew I wasn't on the show anymore. When I was on the American University campus for an event, a student stopped me and said, "I know you must be really busy prepping for this Sunday's show, but could you take a picture with me?" I didn't want to go into it, so I just said yes and posed with him, feeling like a bit of an imposter.

I always appreciate viewers like the woman who did a double take at me from across a clothing shop and yelled, "Big mistake! And I don't watch anymore." I told her that I was trying to be classy about the whole thing but assured her, "You don't have to be!"

I have to admit, however, that losing my job was more than a humbling moment. Over time, I've had to grapple with a real loss of identity. That pain and sense of loss is not something that even my spiritual search has helped me completely overcome. But I know that being grounded in faith and humility from this period will help me find my new identity—my true identity.

I may have been on my spiritual journey for many years, but I have not yet arrived at the final destination. The experience of leaving NBC showed me how much I have to do before I get there. There's a very specific way that I have resolved to change. I want to get better at developing and sustaining community.

I think I could have done more, across my career, to build a supportive network of journalists, coworkers, and friends. I should have been the kind of colleague whom people wanted to stick their necks out for, to stand up for. But in a fickle town and an often venomous business, I don't think I was that guy for many people. Some of my colleagues saw me as just out for myself, because I was openly ambitious and succeeded young. I regret that. When I left NBC, what stung more than the outright negativity was the indifference shown by so many. Many people thought it was par for the course in the TV news business for one guy to go out and another to come in. But it was not a seamless, happy transition. And yet I heard from very few colleagues at NBC. Now I think that if I had given more, perhaps I would have gotten more in return.

Nevertheless, I received an outpouring of support: emails from fans I'd never met and people I had lost touch with from my childhood in California; calls from administration officials and senators; kind letters from colleagues in the journalism world.

One day that summer, after an especially bad pounding in the press, I received an email from a guy you could call the consummate Washington insider. He began by telling me that he once found out through the media that he was being fired from his job running a presidential campaign. No one ever told him to his face that he was losing his job. Then he wrote:

> I learned from this experience three lessons that I pass along to you for whatever value they have. Number one, life isn't always fair, sometimes you get screwed and it's not your fault and it just sucks.

Two, you learn who your real friends are and who your fake friends are and the love and support of the former is a treasure beyond measure for life. And three, the pendulum always swings back, and quality people come out on top, most often even better than before, in ways you can never imagine. You are sharp enough to know all of this and much more, but I wanted to send you this reminder of these truths, and let you know that I'm thinking of you and wishing you the best.

Reading that, I realized I had been given a gift of knowing who really cared about me at a time when it was not popular to care about me. It taught me something about the community I do have. The letter was especially moving to me because this is a guy I don't know very well. He just wanted to demonstrate that he was in my community and was moved to share his own humbling experience in the hope of making me feel better. I'd like to think I would do the same.

The day I left NBC, Erica wrote me a simple note. She suggested that at this tough time, I should put my trust in God and in all those who love and care about me. She closed with a prayer from Isaiah: "I am He, I am He who will sustain you. I have made you, and I will carry you; I will sustain you and I will rescue you."

CHAPTER 7

Doubt

When Faith Falls Away

———————— ✳ ————————

Over years of study, seeking, and desire to know God, my answer to the question "How's your faith?" has grown fuller and deeper. But that's me. And it's the people I have deliberately turned to for guidance. These are people living lives grounded in strong belief. But as I've reached out, I have come upon another set of people— those for whom faith is like it was for me at first: a blank page.

The world is full of doubters, religious skeptics, and antitheists, those who oppose organized religion or a belief in any deity. Some of them have seen the faith of their childhood shattered into little bits by doubt. They don't believe. They don't feel they belong. And they feel guilty about it. They want more but don't think religion is the answer. Faith isn't there for everyone, even if they'd like it to be. You must know plenty of people like this. Maybe this is you.

I asked my friend Salman about his faith. The question tapped in to a deep anxiety he has yet to shake. He doesn't like the question because he doesn't know the answer. And he isn't quite sure what to do about it.

Salman works on special education policy in Washington. He's a gentle guy with a warm, sweet-sounding voice. I can imagine how soothing he must have appeared to the kids he worked with when he was a special education teacher in a school.

Salman's rational-minded investigation into the faith he was born into—Islam—has made it difficult for him to remain a believer. But he is not prepared to give up on himself as a Muslim or a person of God. Though he resists attending mosque regularly, he is saddened by the fact that he does not belong to a religious community. Because he grew up with a strong sense of Muslim kinship in a close-knit Pakistani-American family, he longs for community and simultaneously pushes it away.

Salman is not sure whether God exists, but sometimes he wonders whether he isn't taking a huge gamble. What will it mean for his soul after he dies if he rejects Islam altogether? That thought occasionally worries him. Muslims, like most Christians, believe that there is a Judgment Day on which God will judge everyone based on beliefs and actions. The good will be rewarded with eternal life in paradise, and the evil will be sent to the fire.

Although I have known Salman and his wife for many years, I had no idea how fraught the topic of religion was until Beth and I were talking with them over dinner one night. Salman told us that when he decided to marry his wife, Priya, a Hindu from India, his parents were deeply disappointed. But they were not exactly surprised. His marriage to a non-Muslim was just the latest example of Salman pushing back against his faith.

The resistance could be seen at multiple stages of his life. It began as a questioning in high school and expanded into a more intense rebellion when he grew older. After he and Priya had children, his relationship to his faith hardened in many ways; he found himself resistant to the idea of passing on the rituals and expectations of Islam to his kids. But as he approached his fortieth birthday, he began to contemplate his mortality for the first time and rethink his relationship to God. Is there any relationship there? he wondered.

Salman shares much with others I know who are locked in a struggle with the religion of their birth. The fact that Salman was born a Muslim has everything to do with his story and also nothing to do with it. The same tale might be told of a Christian or an Orthodox Jew. It is important to note this, because it is easy to vilify Islam at a time when we are battling Muslim extremism in parts of the world. Muslim extremism may be one of the most compelling issues of our era, but it is not the only story line about Islam.

I met Salman for lunch one cloudy winter day to have a deeper conversation. We talked at an upscale burger place in downtown D.C., near his office. After I asked him to recount his religious upbringing, the poor guy could hardly eat a bite of his burger. But his tale was too fascinating to interrupt.

Salman Shaikh was born in Lahore, Pakistan, and his family moved to Philadelphia when he was eight. His dad, who worked as a doctor at a Philadelphia hospital, made sure Salman and his sister attended good public schools. His parents quickly established a strong community among South Asian Muslims in the area, through the local mosque and a large family network.

As a child, Salman socialized primarily with other Muslims. Even though his father did not wear a beard and his mother did not cover herself with a veil until later in life, Salman grew up feeling that his whole social and political identity was based around his faith. He spent weekends with his large extended family; several uncles were imams. He attended religious classes at the mosque on Saturdays to memorize the Koran. During Friday services at the mosque, the imam often prayed for their Muslim brothers in conflict in Kashmir and Palestine. Often, at family events, Salman's relatives would discuss the repression of Muslim populations in different parts of the world. Salman wasn't opposed to the sentiment, but he describes it now as an indoctrination that made him uncomfortable.

Salman attended an academically rigorous public school and gradually began to imagine the world outside of his family. He made non-Muslim friends, including Jews. During Ramadan, the Muslim holy month of fasting, he sometimes received an exemption during the week so that fasting would not disturb his studies. When it came time to apply to college, Salman became the first and only of more than thirty grandchildren in his extended family to apply to a school that was not in the area. When he got into a good East Coast liberal arts college, his parents agreed to let him go, in spite of grave concerns about sending their son so far away from home.

Now they regret that they did. "Their worst fears came true," Salman said. "I became the example of what not to do." No one else in the family has gone that far away to college since.

During Salman's first semester at school, he ate an unhealthy vegetarian diet in the school cafeteria, since the meat served was not *halal*, the Arabic word for "permissible." Islam has its own dietary system, like the Jewish system of *kashrut*. In Islam, alcohol is not permitted. Only the meat of certain animals can be eaten, and only if they have been correctly slaughtered.

Salman lost a lot of weight during his first semester. When he came home, his parents were horrified at how skinny he had become. Toward the end of his fall break, they sat him down and said something Salman had never imagined they would say: that he should start eating non-*halal* meat when he went back to school. Salman said they felt they had no choice. "It was probably either that or withdraw altogether." He was lucky that his parents did not ask him to drop out and move back home, but the decision to eat a non-Muslim diet was hard for him, too; it felt wrong. "I'd eaten *halal* through everything, no matter what," he said. "But when I stopped, I did notice that the world didn't fall apart."

That was the first concrete step that Salman took away from Islam. Soon after, he shattered another taboo: drinking alcohol. This, he did not tell his parents about. It still haunts him. In fact, Salman is worried enough about his community discovering the depths of his struggle with Islam that I have changed his name and identifying details to protect him.

Salman was not able to make a clean break with the religion of his birth. He continues to identify as a Muslim-American even today. Salman prayed in college, asking Allah for forgiveness for straying from the strictures of his faith. "During that time, I never questioned the first pillar of Islam, which is that there is no God but Allah and Mohammed is his messenger," Salman told me. He knew Allah would forgive him, he said. He is a merciful God.

In college, Salman did an internship at a center for children who had gone through traumatic experiences. He noticed that they had difficulty expressing empathy for one another but seemed to have greater capacity for compassion for the classmates similar to them. The more he watched how ethnic and racial background affected the children's ability to be kind to each other, the more interested he grew in investigating why.

Then Salman decided to conduct an experiment on himself. He asked himself which population in the world he felt least empathic toward, and the answer was clearly Israelis. So he applied for a fellowship to study and work in Israel for a year.

"Growing up, we were just automatically on the side of the Palestinians. Most Muslims are, I think," Salman told me. "The point of going to Israel was to see whether I could warm my feelings toward Jews."

Man, what the Pharaoh of the Bible could have learned from this guy! In Exodus 1:16, Pharaoh issued a decree to all Hebrew midwives: "When you help the Hebrew women give birth, watch them as they deliver. If it's a son, kill him." Salman had his heart hardened toward Jews growing up, and yet he decided to open his heart to them—knowing that he was going against everything his family and community expected of him. It was an unusual and brave choice.

Salman's trip to Israel was not a vague spiritual pilgrimage. He was conducting a social-science experiment, making himself a "participant observer" in a conflict in which people tend to lock in on a side based on the identity they were born into. He wanted measurable results and thought he might use his experience in Israel as the basis for other fieldwork. Salman admits now that he was also searching for something he had not found in his religious life thus far: an understanding of, and openness to, the different experience of God.

In Israel, Salman took classes at the Hebrew University of Jerusalem. Through internships with Israeli and Palestinian organizations, he engaged with Israeli settlers and Zionists as well as with Hamas militants and Palestinian refugees. To begin with, Salman struggled to feel compassion for Israelis. The proposition was that he could learn empathy, by experiencing the same hopes and fears that Israelis do. But that ability was complicated by how he saw Palestinians being treated there.

Still, Salman found that by making an effort to connect with Israelis, he could start to understand their desires and needs. He was pleased to discover that his skin tone and hair meant he could pass as a dark-skinned Jew. By donning a *kippah,* the traditional Jewish male skullcap, he could occasionally attend synagogue. He could also blend in when he took the bus around Jerusalem. Many of the Americans on the fellowship with him refused to travel by bus because of a very real concern about bus bombs. Israel in the 1990s was not a safe place. For Salman, that was the point.

"Sitting on the bus, I became the Israeli who is looking at the people after him and wondering, Could that be the person who is going to do it?" Salman said. "And I could shift identities, too. If I didn't wear the *kippah,* when I walked on the bus, everybody was looking at me, wondering, Is he the one? I felt the terror of knowing that it could happen at any time."

That compassion, the kind Salman showed in that moment, is critical. C. S. Lewis, the English writer who authored the seminal 1952 book *Mere Christianity,* urged his fellow Christians to do as Salman did: "Do not waste time bothering whether you 'love' your neighbor; act as if you did. As soon as we do this we find one of the great secrets. When you are behaving as if you loved someone, you will presently come to love him."

Salman's parents did not see it that way. His decision

to live in Israel, of all places, felt like a betrayal of his Muslim identity—the family's Muslim identity.

But Salman did not turn his back on his own faith during his time in Israel. On the contrary, he had a Muslim Jordanian roommate, and the two of them fasted during Ramadan and occasionally prayed in the Al-Aqsa Mosque, one of the holiest Muslim sites in the world. However, Salman was challenging the heavy burden of discrimination within his Muslim faith. And this trip was just the starting point. During his academic breaks while living in Israel, he set off on a tour of religious conflict sites around the world. He traveled to India, Turkey, and Northern Ireland, making a point to visit sites of religious dispute. It was fieldwork, but it was also a personal project. He wanted to understand the violence committed in the name of religion—all religions.

"I was realizing that very often there are people who adhere to some truth," Salman said. "And that conflict erupts when others do not adhere to that truth. That's where things started to fall apart for me in terms of religion. My Muslim faith was starting to come unglued."

Salman's scientific, rational-minded approach to the world, by its very nature, required him to question the idea that there is a God. Religion seemed to him to get in the way of a relationship with God: Look how faith had contributed to such violence. He couldn't help but wonder why he should allow religion to define his life.

As he made his way around the world, Salman visited churches, synagogues, temples, and mosques, hoping to feel something, to have some sort of spiritual awakening.

"Did you?" I asked.

"I wish it was different," he answered sadly. "But no, I didn't feel anything in particular."

Acknowledging this is not easy for Salman. Even many years later, the issue of his faith is unresolved. In 1999, on his second trip to Northern Ireland, he met Priya, a Hindu Indian woman who was there for the same conference he was, and they fell in love. Against the wishes of both sets of parents, they were engaged six months later.

Salman's parents told him that they would rather he married a Jew than a Hindu; because Hinduism is a polytheist religion, Priya's beliefs were deeply foreign to Salman's parents. Half of Salman's aunts and uncles refused to attend the wedding because they did not support the marriage. The marriage was tough for Priya's parents, too. They are religious high-caste Hindus who expected their daughter to marry not just within their religion but also within their caste.

Instead of one wedding, the couple had two, one after the other. They had a full Hindu ceremony, then broke for lunch, during which they all changed and switched to another room and a different language before holding a second, Muslim ceremony. Whether to have meat and alcohol at the event was a major issue, because Priya's family is vegetarian, and many of Salman's relatives would not be present at an event where there was alcohol. It sounds like it could have been a Bollywood version of *Meet the Parents*. Salman allowed himself a high-pitched cackle when he recalled the whole thing, in spite of the stress.

Salman and Priya's boys are twelve, Max's age. It's an age at which they have started asking uncomfortable questions about their parents' beliefs. Salman's twins do not identify as Muslim or Hindu. Their names reflect the complexity of their identity: They have Irish first names, because their parents met in Northern Ireland; Hindu middle names; and their father's Muslim last name. With a last name like Shaikh, they are aware that others identify them as Muslim-American. One morning before school, Salman and his boys were watching the news over breakfast and saw that three Muslims had been killed in North Carolina. Initially, the killings, which happened in the winter of 2015, were being treated as possible hate crimes. The boys were shocked and scared to hear reporters suggest that the victims could have been killed *because* they were Muslim.

The report sparked another thought for one of Salman's sons. He announced to his father, "Well, if I die, I want to be buried. Maybe we can convince Mom that she can also get buried, not cremated." He had been paying attention to the ongoing discussion between Salman and Priya about what they will do with their remains. Priya plans to be cremated the traditional Hindu way. She is not deeply religious like her parents, but culturally, she considers herself a Hindu. It's simple for her.

For Salman, the decision is more complex. For years, his mother has been nudging him to make a decision about whether he will be buried in an Islamic cemetery, along with the rest of his Muslim family. The question was whether the family thought it was acceptable for nonobservant Muslims to get an Islamic burial. Recently, Salman's family decided that it was, as long as Salman asked God for forgiveness and began to live an Islamic life again.

Salman is stalling, because he doesn't know what he believes. It's the source of no small amount of anxiety for him. The issue of the Muslim burial holds more than symbolic meaning. If Salman rejects his Muslim identity in a final way, Salman's parents will believe that they have failed as Muslim parents.

"They are worried about my soul, but they are also worried about their own souls," he explained. "Typically, a child will pray for his parents, both while they are alive and after their death. Without that, my parents believe they may not go to heaven. Their own salvation is actually at stake."

Salman almost wishes that he could tell his family to bury him in the Islamic cemetery and be done with it. "But I just can't go through the motions at this point," he said. "If I decide to be buried that way, then I believe I have to observe Islam while I am alive as well as when I am dead. Otherwise I am a hypocrite."

I told Salman that it seemed to me he is not actually afraid of death—he's afraid of life. A life of faith. Many people confront hard questions about their religious beliefs when it comes time to decide how to raise their kids. For Salman, what set it off was the issue of what will happen to his body and soul when he dies.

He and Priya have decided that rather than giving their kids one single religious identity, they will teach them about all of them. At home, they celebrate the Muslim holidays like Eid, as well as the Hindu ones, like Diwali. In 2014 they had a full Christmas experience with the kids. Salman posted the pictures on Facebook: a Muslim and a Hindu and their two sons, posing in front of a brightly decorated Christmas tree on Christmas morning beside piles of gifts wrapped in shiny gold packaging. Later, Salman's family came over for a Christmas meal. The photos show his female relatives in veils, serving a South Asian buffet, and one of Salman's uncles posing with armfuls of kids, wearing a red Santa hat and a white beard.

It looks like fun for the kids. Maybe they are lucky to get to learn about religious belief without having to commit to one religion. Salman and Priya do not believe it is their job to determine their kids' faith. They want to give them the tools to work it out for themselves later. What Salman worries about is not his boys but himself, as he faces questions about death, celebration, identity, and the purpose of life.

For Salman, the answer to the question "How's your faith?" is unsettled. He is not sure where God is in his life. The comfort of his faith life growing up was outweighed by its constrictions. It would be easier if he could just call himself an atheist. But he cannot say unequivocally that there is no God.

"If you set off on this journey and you can't resolve it, then you are left with emptiness," he told me mournfully. "I feel as though there is something shameful about my lack of belief."

Salman is normally a buoyant presence, but he had a heaviness about him as he slowly made his way through his burger in the restaurant overlooking downtown D.C. that day. Watching him across the table, I wished there was some way I could comfort him. "Do you have a yearning for something?" I asked.

"Yes, I do have a yearning," he admitted. "But I don't know if it will come in the form of God or if it will be something else. In most aspects of my life, my path has been to incorporate from others and then build something of my own. I've never been the kind of person just to accept what somebody says is the truth."

"But part of you longs for . . . what? Is it for the comfort of community and belonging?" I asked.

"Yes. For belonging. I don't feel like I belong. I feel like I hide."

Even though there are learned imams in Salman's family, he has been reluctant to ask them to weigh in on his wobbling faith. "I don't know if that's going to give me any more clarity," he told me.

In many ways, Salman's story is more typical than my own. I was born into an ethnic and religious identity that I embraced more fully in the middle of my life. But as Salman reached the middle of his life, he had to reckon with having turned his back on the religious and cultural identity he was born into. He had to acknowledge that he felt burdened by it. He is unsure what this means for him, either in life or after death.

The impulse to reject the faith of our fathers is becoming increasingly common. Some 40 percent of Americans change their religion or give up on religion altogether at least once in their lifetime.

The evangelical pastor Tim Keller has been grappling with these shifts in American religious culture for many years. In the late 1980s, his denomination, the conservative Presbyterian church, asked him to move with his wife and three sons to Manhattan to establish a church for a largely non-churchgoing population. It was to be a church based on orthodox doctrines—the deity of Christ, the infallibility of the Bible, and the need for spiritual rebirth—but it would be in "the land of skeptics, critics, and cynics," which is how others described New York to Keller before he moved there. In other words, it seemed to be what one writer called "a theological suicide mission."

But the skeptics poured in. Keller's first service drew seventy-five attendees; now more than five thousand parishioners attend Redeemer Presbyterian Church each week, at its three New York City locations. The congregation skews toward educated thirtysomething professionals. They come from diverse ethnic backgrounds. Many are single. Many are socially engaged. Some would openly call themselves Christians, though many say they are seekers or skeptics.

Clearly, Tim Keller found a way to appeal to the urban sophisticate. The way he did it was to address doubts head-on. Redeemer's website calls itself a church to "guide you toward growth in your spiritual life." It features a video in which Keller says there is value in taking a skeptical eye to religious belief. This was the thesis of Keller's 2008 book, *The Reason for God: Belief in an Age of Skepticism*, which became a *New York Times* best seller.

When I met Tim Keller, he greeted me warmly. Wearing glasses, a tweed jacket, and jeans, he had a scholarly look about him. We sat on office chairs in a cramped space that he shares with others at Redeemer Presbyterian. In his plainspoken, unassuming way, Keller talked about the different pathways to faith. Before long, our conversation shifted to how religion in America is changing.

"Inherited religion is going away," he said. "Pluralism means that everybody's faith is contested. No longer is the way it was in Europe, where Jews lived in enclaves; or if you were Polish, you were Catholic; if you were Scottish, you were Presbyterian; and everybody you knew was the same."

Now people have to explain and defend their faith all the time—not only in urban centers but in small towns. Keller said he does not think that either Judaism, Christianity, or Islam is well prepared to do this. The major religions struggle to function when their faith is contested.

"Everybody is a little fragilized in their faith right now," he said. "All of our own children are going to choose their faith. That means we all actually have to think out: Why do I believe what I believe? And in many cases you can say, My faith is fine, this is where I am. But I think we should say more often, What can we learn from these others?"

It is the duty of believers to take on skepticism, both that of others and their own, Keller said. "A faith without some doubts is like a human body without any antibodies in it," he wrote in *The Reason for God*. "A person's faith can collapse almost overnight if she has failed over the years to listen patiently to her own doubts, which should only be discarded after long reflection." We should take our doubt seriously, he said. When believers address the objections to their faith, they will hopefully emerge with sympathy and understanding for the other side. They will be able to elevate the discussion between believers and skeptics.

In Mark 9:24, Jesus meets a man who confesses that he is filled with doubts. He says to Jesus, "Help thou my unbelief." And Jesus blesses him and heals his son.

Witnessing my friend Salman's struggles with his faith, I see how much integrity there is in his doubts. He has love in his heart for others. This is what makes him good with special needs children in his profession, and it is why he valued empathy as a student. Salman has wrestled with Islam and with institutional religion in general. But he still feels a desire to engage with something larger and to find the sense of kinship that so often accompanies it.

In Salman's life, I saw some of my own questions reflected back at me. How do I find religious community for myself and my children? Can I find meaning and purpose in the faith I was raised with? Being Jewish is familiar—it feels like family, like home—but that does not mean I am always comfortable in the Jewish community. Though my family's religious life can be complicated, Beth and I share the desire to grow as a family in faith.

When I asked Salman to share his story with me, he was initially embarrassed. He told me he felt self-conscious about his struggles with his belief, because he perceived himself as being in a different place with his faith than I am. He felt that he did not have the answers, whereas I had solved the puzzle. In fact, I have not solved it. We are not so different. We are both in a place of probing our hearts and asking questions.

Salman was open to the strength of experience when he went to Israel after college, and he is still open, even if he's unsettled. Maybe God works like that. I think that the answers, and some peace, can be found in the whispers, just as Elijah heard God's voice not in the earthquake and not in the fire but in the soft murmuring sound. Salman isn't hearing it yet. But through his journey, he has taught me something valuable about the power of opening your heart to experience, acceptance, and love.

CHAPTER 8

Surrender

Let Go and Let God?

———————✦———————

Here's a big question: Are we in control of our lives, or is God? I've never been comfortable with the idea of completely surrendering to faith. You know, "Let go and let God." I feel too much of a sense of responsibility for my destiny. I've also always believed surrender is more of a Christian idea than a Jewish one. But part of being on a journey is being willing and open to learn. And what I have found is that I am deeply moved by the prospect of God being present and at work even when we are not aware of it.

Opening up to God is less of a struggle for Pastor Ginger Gaines-Cirelli than it is for many of us. After all, she does it every Sunday, spreading her arms wide as she stands before her congregation in her robe. She has a wonderful phrase for this: standing in the flow of grace.

"We choose whether to put ourselves in places and

spaces of grace," Pastor Ginger told me as we sat together in her visiting room at Foundry one autumn day, with the last of the afternoon light slanting in through the windows. "We choose whether to serve, whether to pray. And when we do, we are opening ourselves to God's love. We try to be so full of God's love that we overflow, and it spills back out into the world."

But it has not always been that way, even for Pastor Ginger.

In many ways, it seemed she was born for a religious path. Ginger's grandmother in Arkansas would tell her that she was "tuned in to the mystical realm." After college, she got in to Yale Divinity School on a full scholarship. But her spiritual life was actually a mess. She was seriously depressed. Although Ginger had spent her life trying to please others, now that everyone was telling her that she should be ordained, she resisted it. She'd realized that the world was tough and ugly, and she did not want to have to try to make it a better place.

"I know why we use the phrase 'fall apart,' because there was a moment when I was sitting in my apartment in New Haven and I saw all these pieces of myself. It was like I was just shattered," she said. Ginger found herself literally screaming at God. "'I just want You to go away and leave me alone,' I told Him. 'Let me crawl in my hole and live this little cynical, protected life, where I don't have to be compassionate and I don't have to care. I don't want to hope anymore.'"

But God wouldn't leave her. Some weeks later, she had a dream in which Jesus appeared to her as she lay at the bottom of a pool of water. His body was "shredded," she said, and his hands were torn up. He picked her up and they walked out of the water together.

"I was coming back to life," Ginger said. "And when Jesus came and found me, he was showing me the broken places. That's what he offered to me. And it was like: Take it or leave it."

"That life is not without discomfort," I said.

"That's right," she said. "Vulnerability. Brokenness. This is what the world does. It's part of the deal. So you can either live in that world, or you can die, whether you stay alive or not. And that was the closest thing I've had to a conversion as somebody who has been on the journey my whole life."

Ginger was already a person of deep faith, but she'd fallen apart. Thanks to a combination of "Jesus and pharmaceuticals," as she puts it, Pastor Ginger got through that low point. Even though the world is hard, it is also great and full of love. She resolved to live her life trying to stand in the flow of grace. She recited lines by the fourteenth-century Persian poet Hafiz:

> I am a hole in a flute
> that the Christ's breath moves through

"I try to make myself a hole in the flute," Pastor Ginger said.

The classic theological question of whether we are in control of our life or whether God is guiding us brought me to Cardinal Tim Dolan. When I met him at the Archdiocese of New York that fall day, he told me that faith cannot just be a project. It has to be an act of surrender. A leap.

"You're in the process of making the decision: Is this experience going to go from head to heart? Is it going to go from blood to soul?" Cardinal Dolan said. "If you stop at a gut feeling, then your journey is going to be superficial. So you want it to go to the brain. But if it's just cerebral, it's not going to be enough, either. You want it to go to the heart and the soul, where you can absorb it. But that's not a journey that everybody completes. I place myself in that company, too."

"Is it a choice for me to make?" I asked. "Or, if my heart is open, will it just happen?"

He told me that Christians believe that Jesus said to them, "Friends, you haven't chosen me, I have chosen you." He pointed out that this is what God told the people of Israel, too: "I have chosen you." But, he added, "This is where there is a paradox. It's also for us to choose. Ultimately, in the Jewish and Christian disposition, it's always God's initiative. But most people will not allow themselves to be chosen and claimed by Him."

Cardinal Dolan mentioned a painting based on a verse from the Book of Revelation in the New Testament: "Behold, I stand at the door, and knock: if any man hear my voice, and open the door, I will come in to him, and will sup with him, and he with me."

The image in the painting is of Jesus knocking at the door of a bungalow. If you look at the image closely, the door has no outside handle. Cardinal Dolan interprets it to mean that Jesus is always knocking at the door to our heart. Until we admit that things are beyond our control, Cardinal Dolan told me, we are going to be frustrated, lost, and fatigued. It is our job to recognize that we need a savior, and to beckon God in.

"The knock is always His," he told me. "Only we can open up."

At Pastor Joel Osteen's mega-church in Houston, I was able to experience surrender to God on a massive human scale. When I arrived at Lakewood Church on a warm fall Sunday morning, the parking lots were already packed. Sundays at Lakewood are such an event that traffic cops are diverted from around the city to help cars negotiate their way to the nine thousand covered parking spaces around the church. Osteen's church is one of the largest in America. It makes its home in the Compaq Center, the former arena for the NBA's Houston Rockets.

It seems like an unlikely idea to try to create a sense of intimate surrender to God on such a massive scale. But during the service, I realized that being in a mega-church can actually aid the sense of personal connection with God. I was not prepared for the emotional impact of sitting in an arena filled with many thousands of worshippers all singing and praising together. It is powerful, to be among so many people gathered in one place. No wonder a box of Kleenex waits under every chair.

I noticed a father standing near me with his two children, who were maybe eight and ten years old. Even before the service started, the two kids had their eyes closed, doing the praise dance with arms raised above their heads. This family looked the picture of earnest, trusting belief.

Joel and Victoria delivered their welcome message from a stage, through headset microphones, but they were as down-home and easy as if they were speaking to a Bible study group in someone's living room. Later in the service, they invited congregants to come to the front of the church for individual prayer. More than a dozen "prayer guides" appeared, Lakewood clergy and volunteers who lay their hands on the shoulders and arms of congregants who come up front to ask for extra help.

Pastor Joel told me that in that moment, he just tries to give the congregants "some words of hope or faith. It feels simple and feels so inadequate, but you tell them, 'God's got you in the palm of His hand.' It's a moment. They feel touched. They feel encouraged."

On that September Sunday, Pastor Joel delivered a sermon about what he calls "prepared blessings," the idea that if we give ourselves to God, we will get the glory that we are due.

"When God laid out the plan for your life, He lined up the right people, the right breaks, and the right opportunities," Pastor Joel said. "He has blessings that have your name on them. If you will stay in faith and keep honoring God, one day you will come in to what already belongs to you. He is working behind the scenes, arranging things in your favor, getting it all perfectly in place. You couldn't make it happen on your own. It's a prepared blessing!" Later, he elaborated, "I don't believe there's any accidents or coincidences. I believe it's all lined up. I look back in my own life, and I think now that this person led me to this or that."

Unlike some other evangelicals and orthodox Christians, Joel Osteen has a fundamentally optimistic worldview: "that God can heal and help you in everyday life." The words "victor" and "victory" are repeated frequently during the services at Lakewood. His message follows in a direct line from the "possibility thinking" of the televangelist Robert Schuller, whose TV show *The Hour of Power* was on the air for forty years. "Turn your scars into stars," Schuller would say.

But Osteen's belief that God just wants us to be happy has been criticized by other orthodox Christians. Michael Cromartie, of the Ethics and Public Policy Center, compares Osteen's message to a Twinkie—it goes down easily, he says, but is light on substance and will eventually stunt your growth. In fact, Cromartie says if you consider that part of Jesus' message is that we are all broken sinners who must repent, then Osteen's ministry is doctrinally incorrect. Osteen rarely mentions sin, sacrifice, or the need for redemption in his sermons.

"He's bearing false witness about the nature of God and the nature of man" is how Warren Cole Smith puts it. Smith is an investigative journalist with the evangelical Christian publication *World Magazine*. He and others worry that Osteen preaches a version of the "prosperity gospel," saying that God shows us His favor through material wealth.

I asked Pastor Joel about this line of criticism that Sunday after the service at Lakewood. We were sitting on the straight-backed floral sofa in his private suite. Several advisers and publicists crowded into the small room with us, but Joel Osteen seemed to think through my questions earnestly. The political reporter in me expected this megachurch preacher to spin me, but he didn't. He wanted to engage, and he didn't pretend to have all the answers.

Pastor Joel answered the "prosperity gospel" charge by saying that he believes it is only natural to bring God into every aspect of your life, including financial choices. "I'm not saying belief in God will make you rich," he said. "I'm saying, bring God into every part of your life."

"The question that came up for me during your sermon today," I said, "is if God has prepared blessings for us and will deliver these things, then why is the opposite not true? Why won't God prevent bad things from happening?"

"There are forces of evil," he said. "We're in a fallen world. My belief is this: that God has you in the palm of His hand. I don't believe that the enemy or forces can take you away if you're doing your best to please God. We need to trust God, even when it doesn't make sense."

"But is it God's will?" I pressed him. "Obviously, Jews think about the Holocaust, for instance. What about ISIS, the Islamic State?"

"It doesn't make sense, because God could have stopped ISIS," he acknowledged. "God can stop anything. But I think you have to trust that He's in control. This may sound crazy, but if I died tomorrow, you know what? I fulfilled my plan. That's the way I look at it."

"That's why the primary thing that Christians have to do is believe and be willing to be saved, right?" I asked.

"Right. All we can do is let God in as much as we can," Pastor Joel told me.

This is hard for me and many people of faith to accept. God just lets evil exist in the world? How are we supposed to understand that? This may be the biggest obstacle for some of us when it comes to accepting God's level of control.

From what I saw at Lakewood Church, Joel Osteen tries to provide as much room as possible for people to grow into their spiritual selves. He wants to encourage people to believe that God can make their lives better, whether they are depressed, brokenhearted, out of cash, or addicted to drugs.

As it says in Isaiah 42:16: "I will lead the blind by ways they have not known, along unfamiliar paths I will guide them; I will turn the darkness into light before them and make the rough places smooth. These are the things I will do; I will not forsake them."

Joel Osteen may believe that God has more control over our destiny than I do, but I find it challenging to imagine that level of surrender. The Christian message of giving yourself over to an experience of grace runs contrary to much of Jewish teaching. However, I find myself inspired by the Christian language. I have reflected on it and tried to be more open to it.

When I asked the Southern Baptist leader Russell Moore how much God is in control of our lives, he told me that he knows Christians who think it is unspiritual to make any decision unless there is a higher consciousness pointing them in a particular direction. He also believes that God is always guiding our actions and choices. But he thinks of it as more of a back-and-forth with God, rather than waiting for an explicit directive.

Dr. Moore told a story from his own life. When he and his wife were trying to conceive, they had several miscarriages and eventually were told they could never have children. They were distraught. "Even though I was a committed Christian, I was growing really bitter toward God," Moore told me. "I thought, You have all these people who aren't equipped to be parents who are just having babies immediately, and here we are, asking to be parents, and we can't. And I look back now, and at one of those points when I was walking down the street grumbling to myself in that way, our sons were born and waiting for us in a Russian orphanage, and we just didn't even know it. So I see God as sovereign over that."

Dr. Moore said that when he and his wife had to make the difficult decision about whether they should try to adopt, they would pray about it, saying, "If we're going in the wrong direction, God, stop us." They found that people were helping them, and it seemed to them that this was God walking them through that choice. In the end, they adopted two sons, and then three more came along "the more typical way," as Moore put it. "I think of the doctors who told my wife she was infertile every time I go to a birthday party for one of them," he said, chuckling.

I asked Tim Keller, the evangelical pastor in New York, to weigh in on the matter of how much God is in control. He told me a story about a Baptist minister friend who went to visit a sick parishioner. The minister asked him, "My brother, are you taking your medicine?" And the parishioner answered, "Well, Pastor, I don't know whether I am destined to live or to die, so I don't want to take my medicine, because I don't know what God's will is." And the pastor told him, "My brother, I can help you here. I know what your destiny is. If you take your medicine, you're destined to live. And if you don't take your medicine, you're destined to die."

The point Keller was making is that it is not our job to guess these things. "You choose your path and you will be responsible for your choices," he told me. "And yet I don't believe I can completely screw up God's goodwill for my life and for the world. I believe that He is working things out."

That is a comforting thought. It's not that God is 100 percent in control and we are just puppets in His hands; nor are we 100 percent in control and God is just waiting to see what we do. Keller said it's more like 100 percent and 100 percent.

Keller cited the story of Pharaoh in the Hebrew Scriptures. "Pharaoh was absolutely responsible for hardening his heart," he said. "But at the same time it was also God's will that Pharaoh's heart would be hardened. I think God is somehow bearing on a situation so that He is not letting history spin out of control."

Surrendering to God is an essential part of the Muslim faith. On a cold, sunny November Friday, the day of public worship in Islam, I drove out to the All Dulles Area Muslim Society in Sterling, Virginia, to take part in the prayers. The ADAMS Center is one of the largest mosques on the East Coast, serving almost twenty thousand people at twenty-three different centers.

We tend to think of mosques as elaborate buildings with minaret towers, but here in the U.S., many mosques are tucked away into residential suburbs amid immigrant Muslim communities. The ADAMS Center is a repurposed building, so it lacks typical Muslim architectural features. In fact, Friday prayers are held in a gymnasium, a big, echoing room with basketball hoops on either side.

Worshippers wandered into the mosque wearing casual clothes; in the back of the mosque, women whispered to their children, and there was an occasional shout. In spite of the informal feeling inside the prayer hall, the prayer service was full of the ritual of giving yourself over to God.

The imam of the mosque, Mohamed Magid, a Sudanese-born American, strode in, wearing long light brown robes and a matching skullcap. Imam Magid is a memorable presence with a quick wit and an infectious grin. In his robes, he has an air of authority and ease. As he stood in front of the congregation, he recited the first verse of the Koran: "All praise is due to God, the Lord of the Universe; the Beneficent, the Merciful; Lord of the Day of Judgment. You alone we worship, and to You alone we turn for help. Guide us to the straight path: the path of those You have blessed; not of those who have incurred Your wrath, nor of those who have gone astray." As he said these words, the congregation prostrated themselves, bowing from a seated position to place their foreheads on the ground.

The word "mosque" in Arabic means "ritual prostration place." Placing your forehead on the ground displays the deepest humility. In fact, Imam Magid, like many observant Muslims, has a "prayer bump," a dark callous on his forehead from vigorous or extended prostration. It is called a *zebibah*, the Arabic word for "raisin."

"No matter who you are, you can be the king or the president, but you have to surrender yourself to God," Imam Magid told me later. "You say to God, I am always in need of you. No matter how much clout or prestige I have. Each aspect of movement in the prayer is meant to remind and reorient us toward God."

He acknowledged that this act of physically submitting yourself to God can be difficult for new believers, especially those who convert to Islam later in life. He compared it to developing a muscle: It feels unnatural at first; only after a few weeks of making it part of your regular activity will you feel it organically. Once you do, though, he said the experience of giving yourself over to God is quite beautiful.

He told me about an elderly man who had been attending Friday prayers his whole life. One Friday, Imam Magid noticed that the man could no longer bow his head all the way to the ground. He sat on a folding chair at the front of the mosque and simply lowered his head to his lap during the prayers.

"After the service, I asked him whether it felt better

now that he was sitting on the chair and didn't have to bend over," Imam Magid told me. "But he started to cry. He said, 'I miss that moment of placing my head on the ground before God. I want to give myself to Him completely.'"

Over time, I have found myself becoming more comfortable with surrendering to God. What was hard for me at first has become easier. It feels more natural to me now to let Him in, to see God as someone guiding me. I feel as though God knows my mind and loves me enough to urge me to do better.

I hear His wisdom in the voice that I hear first thing in the morning, the "truth voice" before the other thoughts filter in, before I start to rationalize. At this stage of my faith life, I know that God has a daily spiritual ask of me—whether it is giving of myself, avoiding hurtful speech, or controlling anger. Does that mean that God is in control of my life? It is hard for me to get to the place where I believe that God is directing the world for me. I just feel like I bear too much responsibility for what happens to me. Unfortunately, I may hear but I don't always listen, which puts me on the path of the stumblers in life who are always trying to find the way back. The important thing, as Pastor Joel reminds his congregation, is to put God in "first place."

I believe that I am responsible for what I do in the world. If I hurt others, I will suffer for that. But simply believing in God's presence itself is a surrender of sorts. It requires me to let go. Rather than wondering whether

God is controlling me, I try to think of Him as a presence to guide me.

"I turn my eyes to the mountains; from where will my help come?" writes the psalmist. "My help comes from the Lord." My willingness to surrender more of my life to God is part of a larger desire to develop a more spiritual Jewish identity and practice.

One snowy Sunday morning in early 2015, I took my nine-year-old twins to Jewish Sunday school at Temple Micah in Washington, D.C. One of the rabbis asked parents and kids to break off into small groups and come up with an answer to the question "What role does God play in your life?"

I wrote that God inspires me to be better. The exercise made me realize that now that I have studied Him, God is no longer a question for me. Mysterious, sure. But not a question. I know Him. He is many things in the Bible. He is our creator, He destroys, He redeems, He teaches, and He loves.

Rabbi Larry Hoffman says the question shouldn't be whether we believe in God. "Does anyone ask you whether you believe in love?" he says. Like many people, I am lucky enough to *know* love; I don't have to try to convince myself of its existence. And now I am lucky enough to be able to say the same about God.

Now that the sacred texts have become friends to me, I want to relate to them in a direct, personal way. And I feel as though I am developing a personal relationship with God. This is something Christians talk about a lot. Jews, not so much.

I've asked my teacher Erica Brown to explain this

more times than I can count: Why is it that spirituality is not an active part of the tradition for most American Jews? Why is it that most Jews don't think about grace and otherworldliness as Christians do, or about relating in a personal way to God?

Each time I ask these questions, Erica explains that because of the history of exile, modern Judaism has been consumed with the right way to live. Jews see themselves as being agents for justice and decent living. They also have a fundamentally different understanding of the purpose.

"We believe in salvation every day," she told me. "We believe that salvation comes through good deeds. Not through faith. That's not to say that God isn't the fundamental motivation that you do things. But we believe that we have a personal responsibility for our actions and accountability to God."

"What do you think about the Christian idea that God doesn't love us because we're good, He loves us because He's good?" I asked her.

"That's pinning a lot on God," Erica said. "Jews believe that God expects you to do good in the world. That you are His partner."

"But what about God forgiving me for my sins when I stand before Him in judgment?" I said.

"You can only ask God for forgiveness for the sins that you did to God," Erica told me. "If you do something mean to your colleague or act badly at home, God says, 'Don't say sorry to me. You've got to take care of the problem yourself.'"

I asked Erica whether she feels that her own deep faith has given her a sense of certitude and truth.

There was no pause before she answered me. "No," she said. "Not at all. I actually feel that religion has made my life much more nuanced and confusing. I live with ambivalence continuously."

Rabbi Jonathan Sacks told me that Jews were once a "God-intoxicated people." What changed? Too much time in exile, he explained. Anti-Semitism was another factor. Jews have been focused on survival for most of our history, so we have a strong sense of identity and community, but matters of the soul have been less of a priority.

Erica likes to recite an anecdote about her grandmother to explain some of the Jewish history. Her grandmother was raised in a Jewish ghetto in Poland and survived the Holocaust. Erica once asked whether she'd ever been depressed, living in dire poverty and fear, knowing that many of her relatives and friends had been killed. "Who has time to be depressed?" her grandmother replied.

It's hard to imagine Erica's grandmother having the time to sit around pondering what might happen to her soul. And perhaps she partly explains why the Jewish community has not been focused on an active spiritual life.

Rachel Cowan, the rabbi in New York, wishes she could change that. She is part of a small movement among Reform Jews to bring more spirituality into Judaism. She goes so far as to say that there is a "crisis of meaning" within the faith. The cultural aspect of Judaism has become so important among American Reform Jews that it has overwhelmed the other aspects of our religion.

Rachel says many Jews today find it frustrating that

they cannot find the answers to the big questions inside their tradition. At her Reform synagogue in New York, she hears questions like "How do I find meaning in Jewish life beyond community and Israel?" and "What is the spiritual glue that creates shared experience?"

In her own life, she went through a time of desperately needing to engage with God. In 1988, her husband, Paul, died at the age of forty-eight, after battling leukemia for a year, in and out of the hospital. Paul, who was born Jewish, was one of the inspirations for Rachel to convert to Judaism in her forties and enter rabbinical school.

During the year he was sick, Rachel said that she would get angry with God. "Why? Where's God in this?" she asked. But Paul said to her, "Enough of the questions. I'm just believing. I have an anchor that keeps me going. I have my faith and my morning prayer."

When he died, "everything I believed in shattered," Rachel said. "I didn't believe God had caused Paul to get sick, so how could I believe God had failed to save him? And yet even though I know about the Holocaust and suffering, nonetheless my husband did not deserve to die. And he died. So it was like a childlike faith that was lying in pieces on the floor."

Rachel's faith literally seemed to be falling apart. She found she could no longer read Hebrew—"it was like the letters had all separated and I couldn't get them back together again," she said. Whenever she went to synagogue in the months after Paul's death, she would cry and run out. She was angry and confused—why would God let Paul die? Why would He use Paul as a lesson for her?

"I remember walking in the park one day with a friend on a very cold January day after Paul died," Rachel told me. "I looked at the world and I was thinking that all the stones and trees are made of cells. I thought, Everything here is structurally built out of inanimate chemicals, and I got very scared. I decided then that I refuse to see it that way. God in the Torah says, 'I set before you blessings and curses, life and death. Choose life.' So I said, 'I'm choosing life. I do believe there is a God who cares.'"

This was a transformative moment for Rachel. "I was saying, I do believe in this enterprise," she said. "Even though bad things happen, good things also happen; and people are better than they are worse. I know there is purpose for me, even though I don't know what it is right now."

Rachel began to focus on rebuilding her life through a community of faith. She found that she could feel Paul's presence with her all the time. "I realized that I don't feel any less love than I did when he was alive," she said. "And I realized I could make a life for myself."

She began to think about spirituality differently than she had in her first years of rabbinical school. "I decided that I need to have a better idea of God than just somebody that you beg to help you when you're desperate," Rachel told me. "What about joy, what about love? These things had all been in Judaism, but over the years, Jews have said, 'That's what the Christians do. They do love. They do forgiveness. We don't do that.' And in fact, of course, we do. It's there."

Rabbi Danny Zemel agrees that spirituality exists inside Judaism. The Chasidic movement, within the faith, emphasizes the importance of a healthy spiritual life. But Rabbi Zemel says that for the most part, "Jews have been so brainwashed that as soon as you discuss spirituality, they think you're talking about Christianity."

I asked him for his definition of spirituality.

"To me, to be spiritual is to live knowing that God is the witness to every single thing you're doing. If God is here on my shoulder all the time, I have to know that I'm always in the presence of the one and living God. Guiding me, helping me to do whatever it is I'm doing."

"I feel a similar way," I told him. "I seek to operate in His presence. Even though I know I'm constantly failing, I still have a sense of what God expects of me."

"That's important," Rabbi Zemel said. "You can never meet the standard, but the standard is always there aspirationally."

He told me that the word "grace" is actually a Hebrew word, *chen,* which means "living in the constant presence of God." There is a related Hebrew word that Rabbi Zemel especially likes: *chesed,* which means to live knowing that God is a witness and potentially a partner in every act we undertake.

So I am on a search for a new kind of Judaism and a new Jewish language. I want to adapt the beauty of Judaism's four-thousand-year-old traditions to fit a pluralistic society and interfaith marriages like mine a little better. My own spiritual practice is focused on the passion and intimacy of prayer. It is more experiential and a little less focused on laws than a lot of Judaism. It is about creating a spiritual language that will capture the enormity and complexity of an intimate relationship with God.

When I met with Pastor Joel in Houston, he urged me to "Have a heart for God. I would just encourage you to continue to seek and believe that God will reveal who He is in the right way."

Perhaps having "a heart for God" means to be receptive to God's love and His teachings. When the heart is unlocked, it can always grow fuller.

CHAPTER 9

Forgiveness

Who Are We to Judge Our Parents?

———————— ✳ ————————

In Wendell Berry's poem "To My Mother," he imagines a world in which we are able to forgive one another as fully as a mother forgives her son:

> . . . And this, then,
> is the vision of that Heaven of which
> we have heard, where those who love
> each other have forgiven each other,
> where, for that, the leaves are green,
> the light a music in the air,
> and all is unentangled,
> and all is undismayed.

My mother did not have the luxury of working through her feelings about control and God's place in our lives the way I do. She was forced into the place of surrender when she was handcuffed and put in a police car in front of her youngest child. That is what it took for Mom to realize that she was not in control of her drinking or her life. Soon after, she acknowledged to herself that she was powerless over her addiction. She made a decision to "turn our will and our lives over to the care of God as we understood Him," to use the words of her recovery program.

She's been sober since that night nearly thirty years ago.

The morning Mom woke up in jail, her first thought was: I've lost my son. She was sure that I would never forgive her. Our relationship was already fragile. It was different with my sister; we all knew she would never abandon Mom. But there was no guarantee with me.

"I woke up with an ache all over," Mom told me. "It wasn't a hangover. It was so much worse. My first sensation was a dullness, and after that, when I remembered what had happened, I realized I was at the bottom and everything was on top of me."

Mom thought she would never be able to redeem herself to me, and therefore to herself. She felt overwhelmed by self-loathing because she believed she had rendered herself unlovable in my eyes.

"I knew that it would never be okay again," she said. "That's the most desperate feeling in the world, because it's indefensible. There's no excuse. You have to live with the consequences."

In the middle of that desperate feeling, Mom made

a call to one of the few people she knew who had joined a recovery program. As she always says, drinkers know other drinkers, not recovering ones.

Mom found a meeting for a twelve-step program in a nearby neighborhood that night. She still remembers what she wore: a Norma Kamali outfit with big shoulder pads, a wide belt, long skirt, and tall boots. "I looked hot," Mom said with an intentional lack of humility. "But inside was this quivering mass of Jell-O."

She was nervous about going to the meeting. She'd always thought of herself as "not a joiner." And when she walked into the room that night, it only amplified her dread. "It looked like a bar somewhere down in wherever," she said. "They were all scruffy and crazy. I'm thinking, How the hell am I going to get through this?"

But she forced herself to stay. "And then I realized that I was very comfortable. I felt safe. I felt the power of the room. The power of a recovery meeting is overwhelming. If you're open, it will enfold you. I have never left from that day forward."

Once she admitted that she was out of control, Mom wanted to give herself over to the experience. She wanted to be with others who could share in it. She found a meeting the next day, too, in a neighborhood church hall down the street from our house. For years, she went to meetings three or four times a week. She talks about her community of recovering alcoholics as though they are her tribe.

"What I like best about the program is that we pride ourselves on not being gloomy," Mom told me. "We have a gallows humor: Someone will tell a story of falling down the stairs and gashing their head open, and everyone in the room will laugh. It's a release."

My response to Mom getting sober was different. I was fifteen, and I resented the idea that I was supposed to celebrate her. I thought having a sober mother was a basic entitlement. If I could sum up my earliest response to her going into the program, it would be: "Hold the applause." I felt as numb about the end to her drinking as I did about the depths of it; I still was not ready to let myself feel. I was glad she was out of danger to herself or others, but that relief freed up a more vibrant anger toward her.

When she asked Ci and me to accompany her to a recovery meeting to mark her first thirty days without a drink, I felt distinctly annoyed. None of these early steps toward recovery would undo what I felt she'd done to me or our family, I thought. Why couldn't she just have taken heed of the warning signs, and listened to our pleas, and quit on her own without the humiliation of getting arrested?

The two years after the arrest were our rockiest. I shut down emotionally toward her and became defiant about everything from cleaning my room to helping her pack up and move to another townhouse. I went to live with my father.

Unlike me, my sister celebrated our mom's decision and backed her up every step of the way. She took Mom to meetings and joined a program for family members of addicts. But in college, Ci began to have her own struggles. She'd spent so many years taking care of Mom that after our mother got clean and all the initial celebrations were over, she had to figure out how to redefine herself independent of Mom.

I became closer to Mom once I went away to school. I was able to start developing an appreciation for how she had put herself back together. From D.C., I cheered her on. Mom kept some of the letters that I sent her when she was feeling down or abandoned. They were not always especially eloquent, but the sentiment was there. Once I wrote encouragingly about a setback she'd had at work: "God wouldn't have helped you to stop drinking if all that was here was this shit!"

In 1989, on the third anniversary of her arrest, I wrote her a card that began: "Three years ago I sat in embarrassment witnessing the act that would make you realize you needed help. I thank you for helping yourself and for helping us."

I could not possibly have understood just how much of a struggle it was for Mom to stay on track all those years. It is not as though her life after alcohol has been worry-free. In the first few years, there was the inevitable hardship of having to face up to the past and make amends to friends and family whom she hurt. She has had continuing struggles with money.

But within her first year of getting sober, Mom met Jim, a recovering addict who was in the program with her. They were married the year after I graduated from high school, in a small ceremony at an inn in a pretty Southern California beach community, with a handful of close friends present. Jim has been a wonderful and loyal husband to her. For decades, the two of them attended meetings four times a week together. Mom is confident enough now in her sobriety that she is down to two meetings a week. But that's after thirty years of meetings, while living with a recovering alcoholic whom she could talk to during hard times. It's hard to overstate the size of her commitment.

Perhaps the biggest reason Mom has stayed sober is that recovery gave her the gift of a spiritual life. The program reframed her life and helped her develop new habits: Watching herself carefully. Taking stock of her behavior. Noticing what's happening in her head. And praying to God. There's no doubt that attending meetings is her version of church.

"I came to believe that a power greater than ourselves is what could restore me to sanity," Mom told me.

The Serenity Prayer is her mantra, as it is for so many recovering addicts. Mom recites those words every day; "God grant me the serenity to accept the things I cannot change, and the courage to change the things I can" is a portion of it. I think the Buddhist and Christian sensibility in those words must have had a fundamental effect on Mom, because she has an impressively optimistic outlook on the world. In recent years, she seems to have developed the ability to see the best in a situation, even when it is not particularly rosy.

"When I'm at any kind of a crossroad, I ask myself, 'Well, what now?'" Mom told me. "I say to myself, 'What's my next indicated step?' Not what's tomorrow or what's going to happen in an hour. But 'Now what?' And sometimes that is all I can do. From the very beginning, you have to admit that you're powerless over alcohol, that your life is unmanageable. But God, if asked, can help. So whenever you get into situations, you ask for God's help. And it is amazing then what happens."

Mom calls the twelve-step program "a spiritual program on every level. God is everywhere. And it is a spiritual life that is deeply rooted in personal responsibility." Getting sober has brought Mom close to God, perhaps for the first time since she was a child. Now she is enriched by her spiritual life every day.

For years, Mom's faith had wavered. She is reluctant to say that she ever stopped believing in God. But clearly, during her worst years of drinking, Mom had lost track of the idea of God as overseer and protector. It is an understatement to say she was not living with the sense of meaning and purpose that a religious life can bring.

As a child, Mom was brought up believing that "Catholic is the only way. That when you step out of that, you fall off of the earth." She continued to go to church every Sunday throughout her brief career in show business, and even for a while after she married my Jewish dad. The turning point for my mom's religious life came when her first child was delivered stillborn.

Mom first got pregnant when she was twenty-four, and she was thrilled. "I was the best pregnant person you ever saw," she boasted. "To me, I was the picture of a pregnant woman. I wanted that baby so much." But while she was in labor at St. Joe's, the Catholic hospital in Burbank, the nurse informed her that they couldn't find the baby's heartbeat. The nursing staff at the hospital treated her coldly, she says, which made it much harder to come to terms with the reckoning that she was not going to be a mother after all.

The worst part of the experience for Mom was that the hospital insisted she and my dad name and baptize the stillborn fetus and give him a Catholic burial. My mom found the idea horrifying. She just wanted to think of it as a medical abnormality, go home, and try to put it behind her. She and Dad did as the hospital required, though. They named the baby Stephen; my sister, who was born fifteen months later, was called Stephanie in his memory. But Mom blamed the Church for worsening an already traumatic time for her, and she never forgot it.

"I let the whole thing disappear," Mom said. "But it took my Catholicism with it in the process."

After she got sober, Mom started thinking of the stillborn child as what she calls a "spirit guide." Now she says that it was the "essence" of the stillborn child that allowed her to be blessed with two healthy children after he did not make it. Stephen created a "spiritual bubble to protect the three of us—you, Stephanie, and me." She goes so far as to say that Stephen, her "spirit guide," "got me to do the most shameful thing I could do: be arrested in front of my own son so that I could get sober."

In my mom's way of seeing the world, her stillborn baby is always with her. God works through him.

Through him, God embraced her, gave her the children she'd longed for, and helped her to remake her life.

What I see more clearly now than I did then is that when Mom quit drinking, she gave us a gift, too. Ci and I were able to witness her redemption. Mom took what she was and became something better. That is something unlikely and rare. I do not take that transformation for granted. It's a lesson I am proud to share with my children.

One weekend soon after Beth and I had moved into a new house in D.C., I invited my mom and Jim to visit us there. I wanted Mom to see the house and spend time with the kids, but I also hoped to carve out some time for the two of us to sit and talk through what happened in the past and what it means for our relationship today. I'd developed a new interest in revisiting the painful episodes of my childhood. My wife, who prefers to allow the past to remain where it is, thinks I'm a little crazy. I know, enough with the sharing.

Still, my spiritual journey invites me to think about how a deeper faith gives me new perspective on the life I've lived, and can help me reshape my closest relationships. And I wanted to talk about forgiveness. It's easy enough to say we have forgiven something in the past. I believed I had. But Mom had always told me she felt it would be impossible for me to truly let go of the fact that she had endangered me and acted recklessly. I wanted to find out: Had I actually let it go?

This was already going to be a hard conversation. What made it harder was that we couldn't find the physical space to have our heart-to-heart. On the first morning we'd set aside for it, the kids were ranging all over the house, restless between the school semester and camp. They had various friends over and seemed to need access to most of the rooms in the house. Jim was camped out in the guest room where he and Mom were staying.

Mom and I ended up pulling a couple of kitchen chairs into a dimly lit, unfurnished basement room filled with unpacked boxes. She was game to do it—she had agreed—but she was not looking forward to the conversation.

We were both uncomfortable. In my straight-backed chair, I struggled to find a place to put my legs—I kept tucking them under me and then stretching them out again. The physical awkwardness of the setting matched the unwieldy discomfort of our conversation, which veered from the specific details of that day in April 1986 to the hurt feelings of the present with astonishing swiftness.

As tough as the conversation was for Mom, part of getting sober meant she had to get used to talking about the difficult things. In a way, she has been reliving this stuff in meetings for thirty years. She may not talk about it with Ci and me very often, but it is close to the surface for her, unlike for me. That's one of the things you sign up for when you join a recovery program: You live your addiction every day. Most of us try to bury the hard stuff as long as we can—I know I did—but Mom would say that part of what saved her was acknowledging her actions. Over the years, she has parsed them a million different ways to try to extract a larger meaning, and she's given public speeches about what went wrong in her life.

"There's a code that goes along with getting sober, and part of it is that you're only as sick as your secrets," Mom says. She believes that once you name your secrets, you begin to own them. So for her, all this talking is not just worthwhile; it is what makes transformation happen.

I told her that for years, I've felt as though she has been pushing to be closer to me, needing me to give her more of myself. It's all about trying to make up for the past, I said. "You've said many times that you feel you lost me after you were arrested, Mom," I told her. "Do you think you have been acting out of a sense of guilt?"

"Oh, there was always guilt," she responded. "I will never finish regretting that incident. It changed my life completely."

"Mostly for the better," I added.

"For the better—except with you," Mom said. "I don't think you will ever stop being angry at me."

What is the point of going over all this again and again? I've asked myself the question many times. Part of me would love to shut the door on the past. But it kept blowing open. This stuff kept coming up in different ways in my life. It was important to figure it out.

After Mom and I had been talking in the basement room for a while, I got up to get her a glass of water from the kitchen and stretch my legs. While I was upstairs, I took some time to check my phone and see what was going on with the kids. All the back-and-forth was emotionally exhausting, and frankly, I just wanted to think about something else.

Eventually, I made my way back down to the basement room. And then I asked Mom the question straight out. "Do you think I have forgiven you for the arrest?"

"No. I don't think you have," she said. "I think because it's the focal point of who you are today. It's when you got tough."

"You mean you think I hold on to the grittiness that I developed because of living with your alcoholism as a teenager?" I asked.

"Yes," Mom replied. She paused as though considering how much she wanted to say before plunging in. "Frankly, Davey, I have had to think a lot about forgiveness since I got sober. And I think it is used more often as a word rather than an action. But since I've had my faith reactivated through the program, I've realized that it serves no purpose not to truly forgive."

Mom likes a phrase that the program uses for forgiveness—"dropping the rocks," meaning letting go of the things that weigh you down. As part of the twelve-step program, she had to ask for forgiveness from many people whom she hurt, directly or indirectly, during her years of addiction. As a result, she is aware that forgiving is not a simple process, as much as we might want it to be. "I think there is daily work on forgiveness," Mom said. "I don't think forgiveness is the end of anything. I think it's the beginning of all things."

I forgive my mother. I think that I can say that truthfully. The pride I take in her transformation makes it easier. The longer I live and make mistakes as a parent, I'm confronted by the humbling thought: What if my children don't forgive me? I'm doing my best. So was my mother. It's taken me years to get to the place where I can say, honestly, who am I to judge?

It is worth noting that the path was not always clear for my mother to be sober and present in my life and that of my children. Our future is now bigger than our past.

Of all the religious teachings, perhaps the most powerful lesson I have taken away is the idea that if we do not forgive each other, we will not be forgiven by God. I have absorbed this more fully as I have grown spiritually and matured with age. Being able to act on it in my own life is another thing.

Jesus asked his followers to "Love thy neighbor," and he taught them to ask God to "Forgive us our sins, for we also forgive every one that is indebted to us." C. S. Lewis acknowledged that this is not easy to do. In his book *Mere Christianity*, he wrote: "Every one says forgiveness is a lovely idea, until they have something to forgive. . . . 'Forgive us our sins as we forgive those that sin against us.' It is made perfectly clear that if we do not forgive we shall not be forgiven. There are no two ways about it. What are we to do?"

The answer to the question "What are we to do?," Lewis said, is to find a way to love ourselves in spite of all our failings. We must recognize that we are all fallen and yet worthy of love. We must make it our life's work to "hate the sin but not the sinner."

In the Jewish tradition, forgiveness is coupled with active repentance. As my friend Rachel Cowan has written, "Before God forgives sins committed against another person, an individual must seek forgiveness from the person who has been harmed." The idea is that we should be held responsible for our harmful deeds by fellow humans as well as by God.

Only after taking specific steps are you entitled to receive forgiveness. First you must apologize, then you must repair the damage; you must also commit to behaving differently in the future. My mother took all three actions. I do not think that is the only reason I have let it go, but it certainly makes it easier.

Forgiving feels good and makes sense. As Rachel points out, referring to a saying quoted often, "Holding on to resentment is like drinking poison and then waiting for the other person to die."

For most of my adult life, it has been difficult to imagine relationships with my parents in which "all is unentangled, and all is undismayed," as Wendell Berry put it in the poem I quoted at the beginning of the chapter. I think Berry is right that this is easier to achieve as a parent with your own children. As the child, you are allowed to hold on to grudges; culturally, that is much more acceptable than the parent who will not forgive his or her own child.

I felt unexpressed anger at both my parents for years. My mom was the more obvious target. She was forced to accept culpability for her mistakes and to repent for them in a public way, through a recovery program. My dad's mistakes are not as dramatic or easy to grasp. His mistakes were more routine, more like the rest of ours. But it took me a while to find the humility and warmth to see that. At first I just started acting out.

When I was a young adult, my relationship with my dad was about my ambitions. He helped me get my break in TV when I was eighteen: He knew the general manager at the Tucson, Arizona, station where I applied for a summer internship. I sent Dad a copy of my first paycheck to thank him for being my partner at the start of my career. Throughout college, we worked hand in glove; I consulted him constantly on my career goals. During my twenties, when I thought and dreamed of little other than my career goals, Dad and I were closely linked. I'd call him all the time for advice, and he always was eager to help. He liked being able to play a role. He helped me negotiate my salary when I got my second job, at the NBC station in Sacramento.

My dad and I were so aligned that I asked him to be the best man at my wedding, in 2000. When I asked him to do it, I wrote him a note telling him that I considered him my best friend. Dad was very touched. "When you are a father, you try, but you never expect these things," he said.

And yet a couple of months later, Dad and I fought loudly and angrily over the guest list for the rehearsal dinner. I remember pulling to the side of the road in Providence, Rhode Island, where I was on assignment, so that I could shout at him on the phone. This was perhaps the first time I really fought Dad hard, and it began a new pattern in our relationship. Over the next several years, our disagreements grew in number and in harshness as I felt my need for independence growing. I was about to get married. I felt I needed to become more of my own man. I needed to separate myself from him and to make my own choices.

The topic of that first disagreement now seems silly—I think he had questioned why certain of his friends weren't invited to the rehearsal dinner—but in the big picture, it makes sense that I needed to break away from him. One of the side effects of receiving suggestions from Dad for so many years was that he expected me to need him and to heed his advice when he gave it. When I started wanting to assert my own choices, the change did not come easily for either of us. It was hard for me to stand up for myself, and I think it must have been really hard for Dad to take it.

Because I had been scared of my dad as a kid, when I finally worked up the nerve to express myself, my pent-up anger came out in a torrent. Rather than talking to him about my anger, I found myself going after him. It was as though I needed to prove to myself that I could be just as big and tough and scary as he had appeared to me when I was a kid.

This desire only grew stronger after I became a parent myself. I was determined to be a different kind of father than my dad had been to me, in a couple of key ways, and I was self-righteously hardheaded in my belief that I would never replicate his mistakes.

When Max was just two or three, Beth and I invited my dad and Kaye and Ci and my brother-in-law Barry to celebrate Passover with us. It was my first year hosting a seder, and I was excited and nervous. I was intent on teaching my new and growing family the traditions of the holiday. I was starting to recognize the importance of living a deeper, more spiritual Jewish life than I'd had growing up.

I knew that Dad would have suggestions about how to prepare for the symbolic Passover meal. After all, he had hosted many seders, and I never had. But I had a chip on my shoulder about the idea that he knew more about Judaism. I was spoiling for a fight.

As I began getting the drinks together and laying the table, Dad said, "You know you need Manischewitz wine." We'd always had Manischewitz on Passover, so it wasn't surprising that he said so. But I responded sharply. "No, it just has to be kosher wine," I told him. I'd ordered some food from a deli, and as Dad and Kaye and I unpacked it in the kitchen, he said, "Oh, this is just cold sliced turkey. That's not right."

I was suddenly overcome with anger, feeling that Dad was trying to control everything about the meal—my meal—even though I believed I knew how to do it better than he did. I was determined to demonstrate not only that I knew more about religion than he did but that I was no longer the fearful young son. I snapped at him, and our exchange grew so heated that I finally said: "You will not do this in front of my child. I am not going to have this kind of behavior around my son."

Dad left, and Kaye followed him. We had the meal without them. They left town the next day, and Dad and I did not speak for months. Days later, still angry, I wrote him a letter: "After you left, I went upstairs to where Max was sleeping and I touched his head, and told him, 'I will not do this to you.'"

When I think about that letter now, I realize how painful it must have been for Dad to read. And I feel largely responsible for the episode. First of all, Max was upstairs when Dad and I were fighting, so it was not emotionally honest to say Dad was going to scare him while he and I fought. But more important, I was wrong to think I was on a higher moral ground than Dad. As a parent, I had the same struggles with my temper that Dad had, which became clear as soon as Max got a little older. There is nothing in my life that has been as humbling as this realization.

To Dad, my anger seemed to come out of nowhere that Passover. Now I can sympathize. Outwardly, it seemed it didn't take much to set me off. "Why would you say those things to me, when you asked me to be the best man at your wedding?" he asked.

I could have just let his suggestions and little criticisms roll off my back, but I didn't want to let them go. I wanted to use them against him. I didn't know how to calmly tell Dad that I wanted to do things my way. This was our fundamental problem. We never had any practice disagreeing, because as a kid, I seldom worked up the nerve to challenge him. Even as an adult, I felt I needed to yell to get him to hear me. But shouting is not a good strategy to make yourself heard. As it says in Proverbs 15: "A gentle answer deflects anger but harsh words make tempers flare."

Not long after the Passover fight, Erica and I met at Starbucks to study, and when she asked how I was, I admitted that I was feeling a lot of anger at my dad. I was reluctant to go into it, but she pushed me to explain. When I told her what had happened, she said she could sympathize; she had struggled with her parents, too. Like mine, her parents had divorced when she was young. Erica suggested that we study what some of the Jewish texts had to say about living in relationship with your parents.

We talked about the Fifth Commandment in the Bible, which is "Honor thy father and thy mother." Erica told me that in Jewish life, there are two important interpretations of this commandment: one, that you must be in awe of your parents; and two, that you must honor them. You are required to show your parents respect because they brought you into the world. You have to meet their basic needs as they did yours—making sure they are fed and housed. But Erica pointed out that the text says nothing about needing to love your parents.

It was something of a watershed for me to realize that the Bible calls on us to honor what our parents represent in our life. Realizing this about God's commandments gave me a different kind of inspiration to forgive and reconcile with my dad, and my mom, too. It made me think about the fact that I never wanted my children to think it was acceptable to grow apart from me. I want them to stay connected to me, even if we have disagreements.

In that moment, I saw that I had a larger duty to my father, one that mattered more than my anger. After several months, I reached out to Dad and made peace.

Many years later, I found myself eager to explain some of my thinking to him. It felt important because it was so closely related to my Jewish journey, which Dad takes a lot of interest in. I told him that the Fifth Commandment had made me think about how our parents are always the authors of our story.

In my dad's case, I told him, he not only brought me into the world; he helped me become the person I am in the world. He played a primary role in shaping my story. I see that more now. Our relationship is no longer just about my career. It is also about parenting, aging, and a shared interest in our family history. Today I show him the real me including all my imperfections. Like other fathers and sons, Dad and I have gone through many stages in our relationship, but at this stage of our lives, I think we both value being together at all.

I told my dad that I would never be comfortable being estranged from him in the long term, and I admitted the biggest reason is that God expects it of me.

I suspect my dad prefers his own explanation for our reconciliation. He smiled as he said, "What's that old expression? Shit happens. Look, when you have two strong-willed guys related to each other, they're bound to bump heads. That's how I see it."

He's right, I think. It is that simple. Before, I felt I had to go to battle with my dad to prove myself. Gradually, I have been able to accept the ways in which my parents were limited. So am I. We can make life complicated for a while, but in the end it boils down to a few basic conclusions. My dad and I love each other. We had our struggles. Enough already. Time to love and accept and forgive.

One recent winter when Washington was paralyzed by snowstorms, I brought Ava and Jed down to spend the weekend with Dad and Kaye in Boca Raton, Florida, where they live now. On Friday night, we all gathered in their condo with my dad's first cousin Stanley and his wife, Terri, for a Shabbat meal. I made sure to get a bottle of great Scotch. Kaye cooked rack of lamb, and we had challah from the Kosher Kingdom market, which I was excited to discover in the area.

After the meal, Stanley suggested we look at a family photo album he had brought with him. Jed and I joined him and my dad on a big white sofa in the sitting room as they paged through the album. Many of the photos were of the early years of Dad's life in the Bronx and New Jersey. In one black-and-white picture, my father is seated on his father's lap at age three, just one year before his dad died of a heart attack. Dad told Jed, "That's your great-grandfather Morris Ginsberg." Jed said, "He's handsome."

I was pleased to see that Jed was interested in the

photos. He had questions: "What did he do? Why is he dressed like that?" Dad did not have many answers. Because his father died so young, he does not remember key details about him. Sitting beside Dad, I realized what a big hole that has always been for him. I felt lucky that I'd had him in my life, that he had loved me and been there for me, and that he is here to know my children.

As my dad ages, I am more aware than ever how important our time together is. As Dad tried to explain the distant past to his grandson, it was clear to me that he felt it was important to make a connection across the generations. I felt how close we all were on that couch. Family, sitting together and connected by the faded black-and-white images on the page. There was something complete about that moment.

I want to return to the Frederick Buechner lines that I quoted at the beginning of Chapter 1:

> *In these pages, I tell secrets about my parents, my children, myself because that is one way of keeping track and because I believe that it is not only more honest but also vastly more interesting than to pretend that I have no such secrets to tell. I not only have my secrets, I am my secrets. And you are your secrets. Our secrets are human secrets, and our trusting each other enough to share them with each other has much to do with the secret of what it is to be human.*

Why do I think it makes us better to share our secrets? If, as Buechner says, we are our secrets, then we should be able to embrace them, to announce them as part of ourselves. It was hard for me to do that. I spent so many years being protective of my life.

As a child, I was ashamed of important aspects of my life. I held my mother's alcoholism close, not revealing it even to my dad or my closest friends. Later, after Mom got sober and I started talking about her alcoholism, I still longed to develop an identity separate from my past.

One consequence of being self-protective while growing up is that it has taken me a long time to become open to experience or spirituality. I was not willing to make myself vulnerable, let alone surrender myself to God or experience. Now talking about what was hard in my life actually feels redemptive.

It has been humbling to acknowledge my role in my struggles with my parents. It has been very difficult to ask my kids for forgiveness for my behavior. But here's something great that I've learned: There are worse things than being humbled. There is always tomorrow to be better, for all of us.

EPILOGUE

How's your faith?" is probably the most important question I have ever asked of myself or anyone else. The answers we give point to something essential about who we are and who we strive to be. In my life, asking the question has helped me to pay closer attention.

For so many of us, it feels uncomfortable to talk about spirituality or religion. It is one of those topics that we are raised to think of as distinctly personal and vaguely embarrassing.

One brisk fall weekend, I traveled to Chicago to speak to a gathering of insurance executives. They had asked me there to talk about politics, but toward the end, I went out on a limb and reflected a bit on how my faith had steadied me during my tough times at NBC.

Afterward, the CEO of Aetna, Mark Bertolini, came up to me. To my surprise, what he wanted to talk about was faith. Not the conversation you'd expect to have in that particular setting. But Mark told me that he'd had two close encounters with death—his own and his son's—which had changed his life and made him determined to develop his own spiritual practice.

First, his sixteen-year-old son was diagnosed with an

incurable cancer, and although he survived, it took many years of difficult treatment. Then Mark had a traumatic skiing accident that broke his neck in five places. During these episodes, Mark began turning to Buddhist prayer. He found that prayer gave him the emotional strength to start healing physically. He was freed to experience a new side of himself. Eventually, rather than heeding his doctors and going on disability, he went back to work. Today he sometimes encourages his employees to turn to spirituality, if they express a need.

Faith matters to people. So many of us have a craving for a larger inner life, but we resist it. Maybe it feels too raw or vulnerable. Maybe we have trouble with the idea of a higher authority. Maybe it reminds us of a negative experience with religion. Maybe we simply do not have the answers and do not want to search for them right now. But just because we guard our spiritual lives carefully does not mean there isn't a longing right below the surface.

Perhaps there is a lesson for all of us in the Big Book, the basic text of Alcoholics Anonymous: "We could wish to be moral, we could wish to be philosophically comforted . . . but the needed power wasn't there. We had to find a power by which we could live, and it had to be a Power greater than ourselves."

When Pastor Ginger Gaines-Cirelli first moved to Washington, she worked for a real estate association while going through ordination. She moved into a cubicle and filled it with religious artifacts, the objects and books that fill her church office. Her coworkers gradually discovered that she was planning to become a pastor, and one by one, they stopped by her cubicle to unburden themselves about their spiritual lives or the lack thereof. Coworkers she had never met came by to introduce themselves and start talking about the emptiness they felt.

She still thinks about that. "It is as though we are all looking for permission to be more whole people," Pastor Ginger told me. "For permission to say that this spiritual realm, this interior world, is actually a meaningful part of my life."

Since I have started down this road, I have found myself wanting to help give people permission. I am not a pastor or a rabbi. I am not a religious scholar or any kind of expert. But I believe in asking questions, especially the question that is the title of this book.

When President Bush first asked me, "How's your faith?," I was a little intimidated by the question. I had spent most of my adult life on a supercharged path to success. Even when I began delving into a religious life more seriously, I was cautious. I actually believe that my success was an obstacle to my spiritual growth. Maybe it was just that I was too guarded. Something about falling made me feel more grounded in my faith.

Now I understand the spirit of the question that President Bush asked. It was an opening for me to examine myself and my life. Discovering my faith has helped me to see my failings. It has also helped me grasp a new potential for change. In the wake of leaving NBC, I determined to be better. I thought: If I am not different after this, then I have not learned from the experience. I wanted to make it worth something. My true identity, the person I strive to be in all aspects of my life is still to be, is still to be realized.

What I have seen is that God is there when we pay attention to what is happening in our lives. As the theologian Frederick Buechner wrote, "If we are to love God, we must first stop, look and listen for Him in what is happening around us and inside us."

I believe God is working on me, helping me to stand in the flow of grace. But I am not done, by any means. The work doesn't end.

ACKNOWLEDGMENTS

I am most grateful to my wife, Beth, for her inspiration, influence, and her guidance throughout the process of writing this book, in addition to her love. Without her, I wouldn't have gotten this far along the journey. She was also kind enough to let me share details of our life together, which would never be her first choice. Just as important, she was a careful editor, saving me from myself.

My children, Ava, Max, and Jed, fill my soul daily. They cheered me on while I was writing the book, and made some suggestions, but mostly by their very presence, they encourage me to keep striving in all aspects of my life. Ava, in particular, reminds me to avoid taking myself too seriously. Asked if she would raise Jewish children, she recently told me that it depends on how seriously her mate takes his faith. If it's a close call, she said, "We could do rock, paper, scissors; best two out of three."

While still very much a work in progress, I also don't know where I would be in my spiritual life without my friend and teacher Erica Brown. She was an early champion of this book and has played a huge role in shaping me as a person of faith.

I'm grateful to my parents, Don Gregory and Carolyn Surtees, and to my sister, Stephanie Mitchell, for their support and valuable feedback. Reexamining a key part of my childhood wasn't always easy for us, but I feel closer to them as a result. I'm also blessed to have and love my stepparents, Kaye Gregory and Jim Surtees.

In the writing of this book I had valuable help from Miranda Kennedy.

Jon Karp, the publisher of Simon & Schuster, was my editor on this book, but quickly became my friend. I cannot imagine having a more encouraging, nurturing, and patient editor in my corner over the period of years during which we discussed this idea and shaped it into what it is. This is my first book, and he has taught me an enormous amount.

Jon is supported by a great team at Simon & Schuster and that team fully supported me: Associate Editor Jonathan Cox, Associate Publisher Richard Rhorer, Publicity Director Cary Goldstein, Associate Marketing Manager Dana Trocker, Publishing Assistant Megan Hogan, Art Director Jackie Seow, Design Director Joy O'Meara, Senior Production Manager Lisa Erwin, Director of Copyediting Navorn Johnson, Copyeditor Beth Thomas, Managing Editor Kristen Lemire, and Assistant Managing Editor Allison Har-zvi. They embraced me from the start. They also helped me make this book infinitely better.

I was very fortunate to have friends willing to review the manuscript early and give me great feedback, including Jeffrey Goldberg, Meg Herman, Ellen Perry, David Brooks, Jon Meacham, Michael Cromartie, Rabbi Danny Zemel, and the aforementioned Erica Brown.

Robert Barnett, my attorney, provided me with counsel throughout this process and insight into the publishing world, which proved invaluable.

I have learned so much during the reporting of this book and been spiritually enriched by those religious figures who made time to speak to me, in some cases more than once. Pastor Joel Osteen was very accepting and gave me some of his valuable time on an incredibly busy Sunday at Lakewood Church in Houston. I'm grateful as well to my friend and wonderful teacher Rachel Cowan, and Pastor Ginger Gaines-Cirelli from Foundry United Methodist Church. Timothy Cardinal Dolan, the Archbishop of New York, has been a great interview for me for several years, but our discussion for this book is the one I found most meaningful. Russell Moore of the Southern Baptist Convention provided great counsel and insight. Tim Keller from Redeemer Presbyterian was generous to give me the time he did and taught me a great deal about myself and my search. Imam Mohamed Magid welcomed me to the ADAMS center in Northern Virginia for Friday prayers and taught me valuable aspects of Islam. Rabbi Larry Hoffman is a friend who has always encouraged me and has deepened my understanding of my Jewish faith. And I'm always grateful to my friend and rabbi Danny Zemel for the support he shows me and my family.

INDEX

INDEX

INDEX

INDEX

INDEX

ABOUT THE AUTHOR

Over the past twenty-five years, David Gregory's work as a journalist has taken him across the country and around the world. During a twenty-year career at NBC News, he served as White House Correspondent covering the presidency of George W. Bush. He was also the moderator of NBC's flagship political program, *Meet the Press*. David serves on the board of the community-based social service organization Martha's Table in Washington, where he lives with his wife, Beth, and three children.